REPRINTS OF ECONOMIC CLASSICS

MEDIÆVAL ECONOMIC TEACHING

AN ESSAY ON MEDIÆVAL ECONOMIC TEACHING

BY

GEORGE O'BRIEN

LITT.D., M.R.I.A.

AUTHOR OF 'THE ECONOMIC HISTORY OF IRELAND IN THE
SEVENTEENTH CENTURY,' AND 'THE ECONOMIC HISTORY
OF IRELAND IN THE EIGHTEENTH CENTURY'

REPRINTS OF ECONOMIC CLASSICS

AUGUSTUS M. KELLEY · PUBLISHERS
NEW YORK · 1967

HB
79
.025
1967

First Edition 1920

(London: Longmans, Green & Co., 39 Paternoster
Row, 1920)

Reprinted 1967 by

AUGUSTUS M. KELLEY · PUBLISHERS

By Arrangement With George O'Brien

Library of Congress Catalogue Card Number

67 - 28412

Printed in the United States of America
by Sentry Press, New York, N. Y. 10019

AUTHOR'S NOTE

I WISH to express my gratitude to the Rev. Dr. Cronin for his kindness in reading the manuscript, and for many valuable suggestions which he made ; also to Father T. A. Finlay, S.J., and Mr. Arthur Cox for having given me much assistance in the reading and revision of the proofs.

CONTENTS

CHAPTER I

CHAPTER II

CHAPTER III

CHAPTER IV

CHAPTER I

INTRODUCTORY

Section 1.—Aim and Scope of the Essay

It is the aim of this essay to examine and present in as concise a form as possible the principles and rules which guided and regulated men in their economic and social relations during the period known as the Middle Ages. The failure of the teaching of the so-called orthodox or classical political economists to bring peace and security to society has caused those interested in social and economic problems to inquire with ever-increasing anxiety into the economic teaching which the orthodox economy replaced; and this inquiry has revealed that each system of economic thought that has from time to time been accepted can be properly understood only by a knowledge of the earlier system out of which it grew. A process of historical inquiry of this kind leads one ultimately to the Middle Ages, and it is certainly not too much to say that no study of modern European economic thought can be complete or satisfactory unless it is based upon a knowledge of the economic teaching which was accepted in mediæval Europe. Therefore, while many will deny that the economic teaching of that period is deserving of approval, or that it is capable of being applied to the conditions of the present day, none will deny that it is worthy of careful and impartial investigation.

There is thus a demand for information upon the subject dealt with in this essay. On the other hand, the supply of such information in the English language is extremely limited. The books, such as Ingram's *History of Political Economy* and Haney's *History of Economic Thought*, which deal with the whole of economic history, necessarily devote but a few pages to the Middle Ages. Ashley's *Economic History* contains two excellent chapters dealing with the Canonist teaching ; but, while these chapters contain a mass of most valuable information on particular branches of the mediæval doctrines, they do not perhaps sufficiently indicate the relation between them, nor do they lay sufficient emphasis upon the fundamental philosophical principles out of which the whole system sprang. One cannot sufficiently acknowledge the debt which English students are under to Sir William Ashley for his examination of mediæval opinion on economic matters ; his book is frequently and gratefully cited as an authority in the following pages ; but it is undeniable that his treatment of the subject suffers somewhat on account of its being introduced but incidentally into a work dealing mainly with English economic practice. Dr. Cunningham has also made many valuable contributions to particular aspects of the subject ; and there have also been published, principally in Catholic periodicals, many important monographs on special points; but so far there has not appeared in English any treatise, which is devoted exclusively to mediæval economic opinion and attempts to treat the whole subject completely. It is this want in our economic literature that has tempted the author to publish the present essay, although he is fully aware of its many defects.

It is necessary, in the first place, to indicate precisely the extent of the subject with which we propose to deal; and with this end in view to give a definition of the three words, ' *mediæval, economic, teaching.*'

SECTION 2.—EXPLANATION OF THE TITLE

§ 1. *Mediæval*

Ingram, in his well-known book on economic history, following the opinion of Comte, refuses to consider the fourteenth and fifteenth centuries as part of the Middle Ages.[1] We intend, however, to treat of economic teaching up to the end of the fifteenth century. The best modern judges are agreed that the term Middle Ages must not be given a hard-and-fast meaning, but that it is capable of bearing a very elastic interpretation. The definition given in the *Catholic Encyclopædia* is: ' a term commonly used to designate that period of European history between the Fall of the Roman Empire and about the middle of the fifteenth century. The precise dates of

[1] *History of Political Economy*, p. 35.

the beginning, culmination, and end of the Middle
Ages are more or less arbitrarily assumed according to the point of view adopted.' The eleventh
edition of the *Encyclopædia Britannica* contains
a similar opinion : ' This name is commonly given
to that period of European history which lies
between what are known as ancient and modern
times, and which has generally been considered
as extending from about the middle of the fifth
to about the middle of the fifteenth centuries.
The two dates adopted in old text-books were
476 and 1453, from the setting aside of the last
emperor of the west until the fall of Constanti-
nople. In reality it is impossible to fix any exact
dates for the opening and close of such a period.'
    We are therefore justified in considering the
fifteenth century as comprised in the Middle
Ages. This is especially so in the domain of
economic theory. In actual practice the fourteenth and fifteenth centuries may have presented
the appearance rather of the first stage of a new
than of the last stage of an old era. This is
Ingram's view. However true this may be of
practice, it is not at all true of theory, which,
as we shall see, continued to be entirely based on
the writings of an author of the thirteenth century.
Ingram admits this incidentally : ' During the
fourteenth and fifteenth centuries the Catholic-
feudal system was breaking down by the mutual
conflicts of its own official members, while the
constituent elements of a new order were rising
beneath it. The movements of this phase can
scarcely be said to find an echo in any contem-

porary economic literature.'[1] We need not therefore apologise further for including a consideration of the fourteenth and fifteenth centuries in our investigations as to the economic teaching of the Middle Ages. We are supported in doing so by such excellent authorities as Jourdain,[2] Roscher,[3] and Cossa.[4] Haney, in his *History of Economic Thought*,[5] says : ' It seems more nearly true to regard the years about 1500 as marking the end of mediæval times. . . . On large lines, and from the viewpoint of systems of thought rather than systems of industry, the Middle Ages may with profit be divided into two periods. From 400 down to 1200, or shortly thereafter, constitutes the first. During these years Christian theology opposed Roman institutions, and Germanic customs were superposed, until through action and reaction all were blended. This was the reconstruction ; it was the "stormy struggle " to found a new ecclesiastical and civil system. From 1200 on to 1500 the world of thought settled to its level. Feudalism and scholasticism, the corner-stones of mediævalism, emerged and were dominant.'

We shall not continue the study further than the beginning of the sixteenth century. It is true that, if we were to refer to several sixteenth-

---

[1] *Op. cit.*, p. 35.
[2] *Mémoires sur les commencements de l'économie politique dans les écoles du moyen âge*, Académie des Inscriptions et Belles-Lettres, vol. 28.
[3] *Geschichte zur National-Ökonomik in Deutschland.*
[4] *Introduction to the Study of Political Economy.*
[5] P. 70.

century authors, we should be in possession of a very highly developed and detailed mass of teaching on many points which earlier authors left to some extent obscure. We deliberately refrain nevertheless from doing so, because the whole nature of the sixteenth-century literature was different from that of the fourteenth and fifteenth ; the early years of the sixteenth century witnessed the abrogation of the central authority which was a basic condition of the success of the mediæval system ; and the same period also witnessed ' radical economic changes, reacting more and more on the scholastic doctrines, which found fewer and fewer defenders in their original form.' [1]

§ 2. *Economic*

It must be clearly understood that the political economy of the mediævals was not a science, like modern political economy, but an art. ' It is a branch of the virtue of prudence ; it is half-way between morality, which regulates the conduct of the individual, and politics, which regulates the conduct of the sovereign. It is the morality of the family or of the head of the family, from the point of view of the good administration of the patrimony, just as politics is the morality of the sovereign, from the point of view of the good

---

[1] Cossa, *op. cit.*, p. 151. Ashley warns us that ' we must be careful not to interpret the writers of the fifteenth century by the writers of the seventeenth ' (*Economic History*, vol. i. pt. ii. p. 387). These later writers sometimes contain historical accounts of controversies in previous centuries, and are relevant on this account.

government of the State. There is as yet no
question of economic laws in the sense of historical and descriptive laws; and political economy, not yet existing in the form of a science,
is not more than a branch of that great tree which
is called ethics, or the art of living well.' [1] 'The
doctrine of the canon law,' says Sir William
Ashley, 'differed from modern economics in
being an art rather than a science. It was a
body of rules and prescriptions as to conduct,
rather than of conclusions as to fact. All art
indeed in this sense rests on science; but the
science on which the canonist doctrine rested was
theology. Theology, or rather that branch of it
which we may call Christian ethics, laid down
certain principles of right and wrong in the
economic sphere; and it was the work of the
canonists to apply them to specific transactions

---

[1] Rambaud, *Histoire des Doctrines Économiques*, p. 39. 'It is evident
that a household is a mean between the individual and the city or
Kingdom, since just as the individual is part of the household, so is
the household part of the city or Kingdom, and therefore, just as
prudence commonly so called which governs the individual is distinct from political prudence, so must domestic prudence (oeconomica)
be distinct from both. Riches are related to domestic prudence,
not as its last end, but as its instrument. On the other hand, the
end of political prudence is a good life in general as regards the conduct
of the household. In *Ethics* i. the philosopher speaks of riches as the
end of political prudence, by way of example, and in accordance
with the opinion of many.' Aquinas, *Summa II*. ii. 50. 3, and see
Sent. III. xxxiii. 3 and 4. 'Practica quidem scientia est, quae recte
vivendi modum ac disciplinae formam secundum virtutum institu-
tionem disponit. Et haec dividitur in tres, scilicet: primo ethicam,
id est moralem; et secundo oeconomicam, id est dispensativam; et
tertio politicam, id est civilem' (Vincent de Beauvais, *Speculum*,
VII. i. 2).

and to pronounce judgment as to their permissibility.' [1] The conception of economic laws, in the modern sense, was quite foreign to the mediæval treatment of the subject. It was only in the middle of the fourteenth century that anything approaching a scientific examination of the phenomena of economic life appeared, and that was only in relation to a particular subject, namely, the doctrine of money.[2]

To say that the mediæval method of approaching economic problems was fundamentally different from the modern, is not in any sense to be taken as indicating disapproval of the former. On the contrary, it is the general opinion to-day that the so-called classical treatment of economics has proved disastrous in its application to real life, and that future generations will witness a retreat to the earlier position. The classical economists committed the cardinal error of subordinating man to wealth, and consumption to production. In their attempt to preserve symmetry and order in their generalisations they constructed a weird creature, the economic man, who never existed, and never could exist. The mediævals made no such mistake. They insisted that all production and gain which did not lead to the good of man was not alone wasteful, but positively evil; and that man was infinitely

[1] *Op. cit.*, vol. i. part. ii. p. 379.

[2] Rambaud, *op. cit.*, p. 83; Ingram, *op. cit.*, p. 36. So marked was the contrast between the mediæval and modern conceptions of economics that the appearance of this one treatise has been said by one high authority to have been the signal of the dawn of the Renaissance (Espinas, *Histoire des Doctrines Économiques*, p. 110).

more important than wealth. When he exclaims that 'Production is on account of man, not man of production,' Antoninus of Florence sums up in a few words the whole view-point of his age.[1] 'Consumption,' according to Dr. Cunningham, 'was the aspect of human nature which attracted most attention. . . . Regulating consumption wisely was the chief practical problem in mediæval economics.'[2] The great practical benefits of such a treatment of the problems relating to the acquisition and enjoyment of material wealth must be obvious to every one who is familiar with the condition of the world after a century of classical political economy. 'To subordinate the economic order to the social order, to submit the industrial activity of man to the consideration of the final and general end of his whole being, is a principle which must exert on every department of the science of wealth, an influence easy to understand. Economic laws are the codification of the material activity of a sort of *homo economicus* ; of a being, who, having no end in view but wealth, produces all he can, distributes his produce in the way that suits him best, and consumes as much as he can. Self interest alone dictates his conduct.'[3] Economics, far from being a science whose highest aim was to evolve a series of abstractions, was a practical guide to the conduct of everyday affairs.[4] 'The pre-

[1] *Irish Theological Quarterly*, vol. vii. p. 151.
[2] *Christianity and Economic Science*, p. 10.
[3] Brants, *Les Théories économiques aux xiiie et xive siècles*, p. 34.
[4] Gide and Rist, *History of Economic Doctrines*, Eng. trans., p. 110.

eminence of morality in the domain of economics constitutes at the same time the distinctive
feature, the particular merit, and the great teaching of the economic lessons of this period.' [1]

Dr. Cunningham draws attention to the fact
that the existence of such a universally received
code of economic morality was largely due to the
comparative simplicity of the mediæval social
structure, where the *relations of persons* were all
important, in comparison with the modern order,
where the *exchange of things* is the dominant
factor. He further draws attention to the
changes which affected the whole constitution
of society in the sixteenth and seventeenth
centuries, and proceeds : ' These changes had a
very important bearing on all questions of commercial morality ; so long as economic dealings
were based on a system of personal relationships
they all bore an implied moral character. To
supply a bad article was morally wrong, to demand excessive payment for goods or for labour
was extortion, and the right or wrong of every
transaction was easily understood.' [2] The application of ethics to economic transactions was
rendered possible by the existence of one universally recognised code of morality, and the presence
of one universally accepted moral teacher. ' In
the thirteenth century, the ecclesiastical organisation gave a unity to the social structure throughout the whole of Western Europe ; over the area
in which the Pope was recognised as the spiritual

---

[1] Brants, *op. cit.*, p. 9.
[2] *Growth of English Industry and Commerce*, vol. i. p. 465.

and the Emperor as the temporal vicar of God,
political and racial differences were relatively
unimportant. For economic purposes it is scarcely
necessary to distinguish different countries from
one another in the thirteenth century, for there
were fewer barriers to social intercourse within the
limits of Christendom than there are to-day. . . .
Similar ecclesiastical canons, and similar laws
prevailed over large areas, where very different
admixtures of civil and barbaric laws were in
vogue. Christendom, though broken into so
many fragments politically, was one organised
society for all the purposes of economic life,
because there was such free intercommunication
between its parts.' [1] 'There were three great
threads,' we read later in the same book, ' which
ran through the whole social system of Christendom. First of all there was a common religious
life, with the powerful weapons of spiritual cen-
sure and excommunication which it placed in the
hands of the clergy, so that they were able to
enforce the line of policy which Rome approved.
Then there was the great judicial system of canon
law, a common code with similar tribunals for the
whole of Western Christendom, dealing not merely
with strictly ecclesiastical affairs, but with many
matters that we should regard as economic, such
as questions of commercial morality, and also with
social welfare as affected by the law of marriage
and the disposition of property by will. . . .' [2]
' To the influence of Christianity as a moral

doctrine,' says Dr. Ingram, 'was added that of
the Church as an organisation, charged with the
application of the doctrine to men's daily transactions. Besides the teaching of the sacred books
there was a mass of ecclesiastical legislation pro-
viding specific prescriptions for the conduct of
the faithful. And this legislation dealt with the
economic as well as with other provinces of social
activity.' [1]

The teaching of the mediæval Church, therefore,
on economic affairs was but the application to
particular facts and cases of its general moral
teaching. The suggestion, so often put forward
by so-called Christian socialists, that Christianity
was the exponent of a special social theory of its
own, is unfounded. The direct opposite would
be nearer the truth. Far from concerning itself
with the outward forms of the political or economic
structure, Christianity concentrated its attention
on the conduct of the individual. If Christianity
can be said to have possessed any distinctive
social theory, it was intense individualism.
'Christianity brought, from the point of view of
morals, an altogether new force by the distinctly
individual and personal character of its precepts.
Duty, vice or virtue, eternal punishment—all
are marked with the most individualist imprint
that can be imagined. No social or political
theory appeared, because it was through the
individual that society was to be regenerated.
. . . We can say with truth that there is not any
Christian political economy—in the sense in

[1] *Op. cit.*, p. 27.

which there is a Christian morality or a Christian dogma—any more than there is a Christian physic or a Christian medicine.' [1] In seeking to learn Christian teaching of the Middle Ages on economic matters, we must therefore not look for special economic treatises in the modern sense, but seek our principles in the works dealing with general morality, in the Canon Law, and in the commentaries on the Civil Law. ' We find the first worked out economic theory for the whole Catholic world in the *Corpus Juris Canonici*, that product of mediæval science in which for so many centuries theology, jurisprudence, philosophy, and politics were treated. . . .' [2]

There is not to be found in the writers of the early Middle Ages, that is to say from the eighth to the thirteenth centuries, a trace of any attention given to what we at the present day would designate economic questions. Usury was condemned by the decrees of several councils, but the reasons of this prohibition were not given, nor was the question made the subject of any dialectical controversy ; commerce was so undeveloped as to escape the attention of those who sought to guide the people in their daily life ; and

[1] Rambaud, *op. cit.*, pp. 34-5 ; Cunningham, *Western Civilisation*, vol. ii. p. 8.

[2] Roscher, *op. cit.*, p. 5. It must not be concluded that all the opinions expressed by the theologians and lawyers were necessarily the official teaching of the Church. Brants says : ' It is not our intention to attribute to the Church all the opinions of this period ; certainly the spirit of the Church dominated the great majority of the writers, but one must not conclude from this that all their writings are entitled to rank as doctrinal teaching ' (*op. cit.*, p. 6).

money was accepted as the inevitable instrument of exchange, without any discussion of its origin or the laws which regulated it.

The writings of this period therefore betray no sign of any interest in economic affairs. Jourdain says that he carefully examined the works of Alcuin, Rabanas Mauras, Scotus Erigenus, Hincmar, Gerbert, St. Anselm, and Abelard—the greatest lights of theology and philosophy in the early Middle Ages—without finding a single passage to suggest that any of these authors suspected that the pursuit of riches, which they despised, occupied a sufficiently large place in national as well as in individual life, to offer to the philosopher a subject fruitful in reflections and results. The only work which might be adduced as a partial exception to this rule is the *Polycraticus* of John of Salisbury ; but even this treatise contained only some scattered moral reflections on luxury and on zeal for the interest of the public treasury.[1]

Two causes contributed to produce this almost total lack of interest in economic subjects. One was the miserable condition of society, still only partially rescued from the ravages of the barbarians, and half organised, almost without industry and commerce ; the other was the absence of all economic tradition. The existence of the *Categories* and *Hermenia* of Aristotle ensured that the chain of logical study was not broken ; the works of Donatus and Priscian sustained some glimmer of interest in grammatical theory ; certain

[1] Jourdain, *op. cit.*, p. 4.

rude notions of physics and astronomy were kept
alive by the preservation of such ancient ele-
mentary treatises as those of Marcian Capella ;
but economics had no share in the heritage of the
past. Not only had the writings of the ancients,
who dealt to some extent with the theory of wealth,
been destroyed, but the very traces of their
teaching had been long forgotten. A good
example of the state of thought in economic
matters is furnished by the treatment which
money receives in the *Etymologies* of Isidore of
Seville, which was regarded in the early Middle
Ages as a reliable encyclopædia. ' Money,' according to Isidore, ' is so called because it warns,
monet, lest any fraud should enter into its com-
position or its weight. The piece of money is
the coin of gold, silver, or bronze, which is called
nomisma, because it bears the imprint of the
name and likeness of the prince. . . . The pieces
of money *nummi* have been so called from the
King of Rome, Numa, who was the first among
the Latins to mark them with the imprint of his
image and name.' [1] Is it any wonder that the
early Middle Ages were barren of economic
doctrines, when this was the best instruction to
which they had access ?

In the course of the thirteenth century a great
change occurred. The advance of civilisation,
the increased organisation of feudalism, the
development of industry, and the extension of
commerce, largely under the influence of the
Crusades, all created a condition of affairs in which

[1] *Etymol.*, xvi. 17.

economic questions could no longer be overlooked or neglected.   At the same time the
renewed study of the writings of Aristotle served
to throw a flood of new light on the nature of
wealth.

The *Ethics* and *Politics* of Aristotle, although
they are not principally devoted to a treatment of
the theory of wealth, do in fact deal with that
subject incidentally.   Two points in particular
are touched on, the utility of money and the
injustice of usury.   The passages of the philosopher dealing with these subjects are of particular interest, as they may be said, with a good
deal of truth, to be the true starting point of
mediæval economics.[1]   The writings of Aristotle
arrested the attention, and aroused the admiration of the theologians of the thirteenth century ;
and it would be quite impossible to exaggerate
the influence which they exercised on the later
development of mediæval thought.   Albertus
Magnus digested, interpreted, and systematised
the whole of the works of the Stagyrite ; and was
so steeped in the lessons of his philosophic master
as to be dubbed by some ' the ape of Aristotle.'
Aquinas, who was a pupil of Albertus, also studied
and commented on Aristotle, whose aid he was
always ready to invoke in the solution of all his
difficulties.   With the single and strange exception of Vincent de Beauvais, Aristotle's teaching
on money was accepted by all the writers of the
thirteenth century, and was followed by later
generations.[2]   The influence of Aristotle is appar-

[1] Jourdain, *op. cit.*, p. 7.   [2] *Ibid.*, p. 12.

ent in every article of the *Summa*, which was itself the starting point from which all discussion sprang for the following two centuries ; and it is not too much to say that the Stagyrite had a decisive influence on the introduction of economic notions into the controversies of the Schools. ' We find in the writings of St. Thomas Aquinas,' says Ingram, ' the economic doctrines of Aristotle reproduced with a partial infusion of Christian elements.' [1]

In support of the account we have given of the development of economic thought in the thirteenth century, we may quote Cossa : ' The revival of economic studies in the Middle Ages only dates from the thirteenth century. It was due in a great measure to a study of the *Ethics* and *Politics* of Aristotle, whose theories on wealth were paraphrased by a considerable number of commentators. Before that period we can only find moral and religious dissertations on such topics as the proper use of material goods, the dangers of luxury, and undue desire for wealth. This is easily explained when we take into consideration (1) the prevalent influence of religious ideas at the time, (2) the strong reaction against the materialism of pagan antiquity, (3) the predominance of natural economy, (4) the small importance of international trade, and (5) the decay of the profane sciences, and the metaphysical tendencies of the more solid thinkers of the Middle Ages.' [2]

[1] *Op. cit.*, p. 27. Espinas thinks that the influence of Aristotle in this respect has been exaggerated. (*Histoire des Doctrines Économiques*, p. 80.)

[2] *Op. cit.*, p. 14 ; Espinas, *op. cit.*, p. 80.

The teaching of Aquinas upon economic affairs remained the groundwork of all the later writers until the end of the fifteenth century. His opinions on various points were amplified and explained by later authors in more detail than he himself employed; monographs of considerable length were devoted to the treatment of questions which he dismissed in a single article; but the development which took place was essentially one of amplification rather than opposition. The monographists of the later fifteenth century treat usury and sale in considerable detail; many refinements are indicated which are not to be found in the *Summa*; but it is quite safe to say that none of these later writers ever pretended to supersede the teaching of Aquinas, who was always admitted to be the ultimate authority. ' During the fourteenth and fifteenth centuries, the general political doctrine of Aquinas was maintained with merely subordinate modifications.' [1] ' The canonist doctrine of the fifteenth century,' according to Sir William Ashley, ' was but a development of the principles to which the Church had already given its sanction in earlier centuries. It was the outcome of these same principles working in a modified environment. But it may more fairly be said to present a *system* of economic thought, because it was no longer a collection of unrelated opinions, but a connected whole. The tendency towards a separate department of study is shown by the ever-increasing space devoted to the discussion of general economic topics in

[1] Ingram, *op. cit.*, p. 35.

general theological treatises, and more notably
still in the manuals of casuistry for the use of the
confessional, and handbooks of canon law for
the use of ecclesiastical lawyers. It was shown
even more distinctly by the appearance of a shoal
of special treatises on such subjects as contracts,
exchange, and money, not to mention those on
usury.' [1] In all this development, however, the
principles enunciated by Aquinas, and through
him, by Aristotle, though they may have been
illustrated and applied to new instances, were
never rejected. The study of the writers of this
period is therefore the study of an organic whole,
the germ of which is to be found in the writings of
Aquinas.[2]

§ 3. *Teaching*

We shall confine our attention in this essay to
the economic teaching of the Middle Ages, and
shall not deal with the actual practice of the
period. It may be objected that a study of the
former without a study of the latter is futile and

[1] *Op. cit.,* vol. i. pt. ii. p. 382.

[2] The volume of literature which bears more or less on economic
matters dating from the fourteenth and fifteenth centuries is colossal.
By far the best account of it is to be found in Endemann's *Studien in
der Romanisch-canonistischen Wirthschafts- und Rechtslehre,* vol. i.
pp. 25 *et seq.* Many of the more important works written during the
period are reprinted in the *Tractatus Universi Juris,* vols. vi. and vii.
The appendix to the first chapter of Roscher's *Geschichte* also contains
a valuable account of certain typical writers, especially of Langenstein
and Henricus de Hoyta. Brants gives a useful bibliographical list of
both mediæval and modern authorities in the second chapter of his
Théories économiques aux xiii et xiv* siècles.* Those who desire further
information about any particular writer of the period will find it in

useless ; that the economic teaching of a period
can only be satisfactorily learnt from a study
of its actual economic institutions and customs;
and that the scholastic teaching was nothing
but a casuistical attempt to reconcile the early
Christian dogmas with the ever-widening exigencies
of real life. Endemann, for instance, devotes a
great part of his invaluable books on the subject
to demonstrating how impracticable the canonist
teaching was when it was applied to real life,
and recounting the casuistical devices that were
resorted to in order to reconcile the teaching of
the Church with the accepted mercantile customs
of the time. Endemann, however, in spite of his
colossal research and unrivalled acquaintance
with original authorities, was essentially hostile
to the system which he undertook to explain, and
thus lacked the most essential quality of a satisfactory expositor, namely, sympathy with his
subject. He does not appear to have realised
that development and adaptability to new situa-
tions, far from being marks of impracticability,
are rather the signs of vitality and of elasticity.
This is not the place to discuss how far the
doctrine of the late fifteenth differed from that of
the early thirteenth century ; that is a matter
which will appear below when each of the leading

Stintzing, *Literaturgeschichte des röm. Rechts*, or in Chevallier's *Réper-
toire historique des Sources du moyen âge* ; *Bio-bibliographie*. The
authorship of the treatise *De Regimine Principum*, from which we shall
frequently quote, often attributed to Aquinas, is very doubtful. The
most probable opinion is that the first book and the first three
chapters of the second are by Aquinas, and the remainder by another
writer. (See Franck, *Réformateurs et Publicistes*, vol. i. p. 83.)

principles of scholastic economic teaching is separately considered ; it is sufficient to say here that we agree entirely with Brants, in opposition to Endemann, that the change which took place in the interval was one of development, and not of opposition. ' The law,' says Brants, ' remained identical and unchanged ; justice and charity—nobody can justly enrich himself at the expense of his neighbour or of the State, but the reasons justifying gain are multiplied according as riches are developed.' [1] ' The canonist doctrine of the fifteenth century was but a development of the principles to which the Church had already given its sanction in earlier centuries. It was the outcome of these same principles working in a modified environment.' [2] With these conclusions of Brants and Ashley we are in entire agreement.

Let us say in passing that the assumption that the mediæval teaching grew out of contemporary practice, rather than that the latter grew out of the former, is one which does not find acceptance among the majority of the students of the subject. The problem whether a correct understanding of mediæval economic life can be best attained by first studying the teaching or the practice is possibly no more soluble than the old riddle of the hen and the egg ; but it may at least be argued that there is a good deal to be said on both sides. The supporters of the view that practice moulded theory are by no means unopposed. There is no doubt that in many respects the

[1] Brants, *op. cit.*, p. 9.　　　　[2] Ashley, *op. cit.*, p. 381.

exigencies of everyday commercial concerns came
into conflict with the tenets of canon law and
scholastic opinion ; but the admission of this
fact does not at all prove that the former was the
element which modified the latter, rather than
the latter the former. In so far as the expansion
of commerce and the increasing complexity of
intercourse raised questions which seemed to
indicate that mercantile convenience conflicted
with received teaching, it is probable that the
difficulty was not so much caused by a contradiction between the former and the latter, as by
the fact that an interpretation of the doctrine
as applied to the facts of the new situation was
not available before the new situation had actually
arisen. This is a phenomenon frequently met with
at the present day in legal practice ; but no
lawyer would dream of asserting that, because
there had arisen an unprecedented state of facts,
to which the application of the law was a matter
of doubt or difficulty, therefore the law itself was
obsolete or incomplete. Examples of such a
conflict are familiar to any one who has ever
studied the case law on any particular subject,
either in a country such as England, where the
law is unwritten, or in continental countries,
where the most exhaustive and complete codes
have been framed. Nevertheless, in spite of the
occurrence of such difficulties, it would be foolish
to contend that the laws in force for the time being
have not a greater influence on the practice of
mercantile transactions than the convenience of
merchants has upon the law. How much more

potent must this influence have been when the law did not apply simply to outward observances, but to the inmost recesses of the consciences of believing Christians!

The opinion that mediæval teaching exercised a profound effect on mediæval practice is supported by authorities of the weight of Ashley, Ingram, and Cunningham,[1] the last of whom was in some respects unsympathetic to the teaching the influence of which he rates so highly. 'It has indeed,' writes Sir William Ashley, 'not infrequently been hinted that all the elaborate argumentation of canonists and theologians was "a cobweb of the brain," with no vital relation to real life. Certain German writers have, for instance, maintained that, alongside of the canonist doctrine with regard to trade, there existed in mediæval Europe a commercial law, recognised in the secular courts, and altogether opposed to the peculiar doctrines of the canonists. It is true that parts of mercantile jurisprudence, such as the law of partnership, had to a large extent originated in the social conditions of the time, and would have probably made their appearance even if there had been no canon law or theology. But though there were branches of commercial law which were, in the main, independent of the canonist doctrine, there were none that were opposed to it. On the fundamental points of usury and just price, commercial law in the later Middle Ages adopted com-

---

[1] Even Endemann warns his readers against assuming that the canonist teaching had no influence on everyday life. (*Studien*, vol. ii. p. 404.)

pletely the principles of the canonists. How entirely these principles were recognised in the practice of the courts which had most to do with commercial suits, viz. those of the towns, is sufficiently shown by the frequent enactments as to usury and as to reasonable price which are found in the town ordinances of the Middle Ages ; in England as well as in the rest of Western Europe. . . . Whatever may have been the effect, direct or indirect, of the canonist doctrine on legislation, it is certain that on its other side, as entering into the moral teaching of the Church through the pulpit and the confessional, its influence was general and persistent, even if it were not always completely successful.' [1] ' Every great change of opinion on the destinies of man,' says Ingram, ' and the guiding principles of conduct must react in the sphere of material interests ; and the Catholic religion had a profound influence on the economic life of the Middle Ages. . . . The constant presentations to the general mind and conscience of Christian ideas, the dogmatic bases of which were as yet scarcely assailed by scepticism, must have had a powerful effect in moralising life.' [2] According to Dr. Cunningham : ' The mediæval doctrine of price was not a theory intended to explain the phenomena of society, but it was laid down as the basis of rules which should control the conduct of society and of individuals. At the same time current opinion seems to have

---

[1] Ashley, op. cit., vol. i. pt. ii. pp. 383-85. Again : ' The later canonist dialectic was the midwife of modern economics ' (ibid., p. 397).

[2] History of Political Economy, p. 26.

been so fully formed in accordance with it that a
brief enumeration of the doctrine of a just price
will serve to set the practice of the day in clearer
light. In regard to other matters, it is difficult
to determine how far public opinion was swayed
by practical experience, and how far it was really
moulded by Christian teaching—this is the case
in regard to usury. But there can be little doubt
about the doctrine of price—which really under-
lies a great deal of commercial and gild regulations,
and is constantly implied in the early legislation
on mercantile affairs.' [1] The same author expresses the same opinion in another work : ' The
Christian doctrine of price, and Christian condemnation of gain at the expense of another man,
affected all the mediæval organisation of municipal
life and regulation of inter-municipal commerce,
and introduced marked contrasts to the conditions
of business in ancient cities. The Christian appreciation of the duty of work rendered the lot
of the mediæval villain a very different thing
from that of the slave of the ancient empire. The
responsibility of proprietors, like the responsibility
of prices, was so far insisted on as to place sub-
stantial checks on tyranny of every kind. For
these principles were not mere pious opinions, but
effective maxims in practical life. Owing to the
circumstances in which the vestiges of Roman
civilisation were locally maintained, and the
foundations of the new society were laid, there
was ample opportunity for Christian teaching and

[1] Cunningham, *Growth of English Industry and Commerce*, vol. i.
p. 252.

example to have a marked influence on its development.'[1] In Dr. Cunningham's book entitled *Politics and Economics* the same opinion is expressed :[2] 'Religious and industrial life were closely interconnected, and there were countless points at which the principles of divine law must have been brought to bear on the transaction of business, altogether apart from any formal tribunal. Nor must we forget the opportunities which directors had for influencing the conduct of penitents. . . . Partly through the operation of the royal power, partly through the decisions of ecclesiastical authorities, but more generally through the influence of a Christian public opinion which had been gradually created, the whole industrial organism took its shape, and the acknowledged economic principles were framed.'

We have quoted these passages from Dr. Cunningham's works at length because they are of great value in helping us to estimate the rival parts played by theory and practice in mediæval economic teaching ; in the first place, because the author was by no means prepossessed in favour of the teaching of the canonists, but rather unsympathetic to it ; in the second place, because, although his work was concerned primarily with practice, he found himself obliged to make a study of theory before he could properly understand the practice ; and lastly, because they point particularly to the effect of the teaching on just price. When we come to speak of this part of the subject

[1] Cunningham, *Western Civilisation*, vol. ii. pp. 9-10.
[2] P. 25.

we shall find that Dr. Cunningham failed to appreciate the true significance of the canonist doctrine. If an eminent author, who does not quite appreciate the full import of this doctrine, and who is to some extent contemptuous of its practical value, nevertheless asserts that it exercised an all-powerful influence on the practice of the age in which it was preached, we are surely justified in asserting that the study of theory may be profitably pursued without a preliminary history of the contemporary practice.

But we must not be taken to suggest that there were no conflicts between the teaching and the practice of the Middle Ages. As we have seen, the economic teaching of that period was ethical, and it would be absurd to assert that every man who lived in the Middle Ages lived up to the high standard of ethical conduct which was proposed by the Church.[1] One might as well say that stealing was an unknown crime in England since the passing of the Larceny Act. All we do suggest is that the theory had such an important and incalculable influence upon practice that the study of it is not rendered futile or useless because of occasional or even frequent departures from it in real life. Even Endemann says : ' The teach-

[1] The many devices which were resorted to in order to evade the prohibition of usury are explained in Dr. Cunningham's *Growth of English Industry and Commerce*, vol. i. p. 255. See also Delisle, *L'Administration financière des Templiers*, Académie des Inscriptions et Belles-Lettres, 1889, vol. xxxiii. pt. ii., and Ashley, *Economic History*, vol. i. pt. ii. p. 426. The *Summa Pastoralis* of Raymond de Pennafort analyses and demolishes many of the commoner devices which were employed to evade the usury laws. On the part played by the Jews, see Brants, *op. cit.*, Appendix I.

ing of the canon law presents a noble edifice not
less splendid in its methods than in its results.
It embraces the whole material and spiritual
natures of human society with such power and
completeness that verily no room is left for any
other life than that decreed by its dogmas.'[1]
' The aim of the Church,' says Janssen, ' in view
of the tremendous agencies through which it
worked, in view of the dominion which it really
exercised, cannot have the impression of its great-
ness effaced by the unfortunate fact that all was
not accomplished that had been planned.'[2]   The
fact that tyranny may have been exercised by
some provincial governor in an outlying island of
the Roman Empire cannot close our eyes to the
benefits to be derived from a study of the code
of Justinian ; nor can a remembrance of the
manner in which English law is administered in
Ireland in times of excitement, blind us to the
political lessons to be learned from an examination of the British constitution.

Section 3.—Value of the Study of the Subject

The question may be asked whether the study
of a system of economic teaching, which, even if
it ever did receive anything approaching universal
assent, has long since ceased to do so, is not a
waste of labour. We can answer that question
in the negative, for two reasons. In the first
place, as we said above, a proper understanding

[1] *Die Nationalökonomischen Grundsätze der canonistischen Lehre*,
p. 192.   [2] *History of the German People* (Eng. trans.), vol. ii. p. 99.

of the earlier periods of the development of a
body of knowledge is indispensable for a full
appreciation of the later. Even if the canonist
system were not worth studying for its own sake,
it would be deserving of attention on account of
the light it throws on the development of later
economic doctrine. ' However the canonist theory
may contrast with or resemble modern economics,
it is too important a part of the history of human
thought to be disregarded,' says Sir William
Ashley. ' As we cannot fully understand the work
of Adam Smith without giving some attention to
the physiocrats, nor the physiocrats without
looking at the mercantilists : so the beginnings
of mercantile theory are hardly intelligible without
a knowledge of the canonist doctrine towards
which that theory stands in the relation partly
of a continuation, partly of a protest.' [1]

But we venture to assert that the study of
canonist economics, far from being useful simply
as an introduction to later theories, is of great
value in furnishing us with assistance in the
solution of the economic and social problems of the
present day. The last fifty years have witnessed
a reaction against the scientific abstractions of the
classical economists, and modern thinkers are
growing more and more dissatisfied with an
economic science which leaves ethics out of
account.[2] Professor Sidgwick, in his *Principles*

---

[1] *Op. cit.*, vol. i. pt. ii. p. 381.

[2] We must guard against the error, which is frequently made, that,
because the classical economists assumed self-interest as the sole motive
of economic action, they therefore approved of and inculcated it.

of Political Economy, published in 1883, devotes
a separate section to 'The Art of Political Economy,' in which he remarks that ' The principles
of Political Economy are still most commonly
understood even in England, and in spite of many
protests to the contrary, to be practical principles
—rules of conduct, public or private.'[1] The many
indications in recent literature and practice that
the regulation of prices should be controlled by
principles of ' fairness ' would take too long to
recite. It is sufficient to refer to the conclusion
of Devas on this point : ' The notion of just price,
worked out in detail by the theologians, and in
later days rejected as absurd by the classical
economists, has been rightly revived by modern
economists.'[2] Not alone in the sphere of price,
but in that of every other department of economics,
the impossibility of treating the subject as an
abstract science without regard to ethics is being
rapidly abandoned. ' The best usage of the
present time,' according to the *Catholic Encyclopædia,* ' is to make political economy an ethical
science—that is, to make it include a discussion of
what ought to be in the economic world as well
as what is.'[3] We read in the 1917 edition of
Palgrave's *Dictionary of Political Economy,* that
' The growing importance of distribution as a
practical problem has led to an increasing mutual
interpenetration of economic and ethical ideas,
which in the development of economic doctrine

---

[1] P. 401, and see Marshall's Preface to Price's *Industrial Peace,*
and Ashley, *op. cit.,* vol. i. pt. i. p. 137.

[2] *Political Economy,* p. 268.   [3] Tit., ' Political Economy.'

during the last century and a half has taken various forms.'[1] The need for some principle by which just distribution can be attained has been rendered pressing by the terrible effects of a period of unrestricted competition. ' It has been widely maintained that a strictly competitive exchange does not tend to be really fair—some say cannot be really fair—when one of the parties is under pressure of urgent need ; and further, that the inequality of opportunity which private property involves cannot be fully justified on the principle of maintaining equal freedom, and leads, in fact, to grave social injustice.'[2] In other words, the present condition of affairs is admitted to be intolerable, and the task before the world is to discover some alternative. The day when economics can be divorced from ethics has passed away ; there is a world-wide endeavour to establish in the place of the old, a new society founded on an ethical basis.[3] There are two, and only two, possible ways to the attainment of this ideal— the way of socialism and the way of Christianity.

There can be no doubt the socialist movement derives a great part of its popularity from its promise of a new order, based, not on the unregulated pursuit of selfish desires, but on justice. ' To this view of justice or equity,' writes Dr. Sidgwick, ' the socialistic contention that labour can only receive its due reward if land and other instruments of production are taken into public

---

[1] Vol. iii. p. 138.   [2] Ibid.
[3] See Laveleye, Elements of Political Economy (Eng. trans.), pp. 7-8. On the general conflict between the ethical and the non-ethical schools of economists see Keynes, Scope and Method, pp. 20 et seq.

ownership, and education of all kinds gratuitously provided by Government—has powerfully
appealed ; and many who are not socialists, nor
ignorant of economic science, have been led by
it to give welcome to the notion that the ideally
" fair " price of a productive service is a price at
least rendering possible the maintenance of the
producers and their families in a condition of
health and industrial efficiency.' This is not the
place to enter into a discussion as to the merits
or practicability of any of the numerous schemes
put forward by socialists ; it is sufficient to say
that socialism is essentially unhistorical, and that
in our opinion any practical benefits which it
might bestow on society would be more than
counterbalanced by the innumerable evils which
would be certain to emerge in a system based on
unsatisfactory foundations.

The other road to the establishment of a society
based on justice is the way of Christianity, and,
if we wish to attempt this path, it becomes
vitally important to understand what was the
economic teaching of the Church in the period
when the Christian ethic was universally recognised.   During the whole Middle Ages, as we have
said above, the Canon Law was the test of right
and wrong in the domain of economic activity ;
production, consumption, distribution, and exchange were all regulated by the universal system
of law ; once before economic life was considered
within the scope of moral regulation.   It cannot
be denied that a study of the principles which were
accepted during that period may be of great

value to a generation which is striving to place its economic life once more upon an ethical foundation. One error in particular we must be on our guard to avoid. We said above that both the socialists and the Christian economists are agreed in their desire to reintroduce justice into economic life. We must not conclude, however, that the aims of these two schools are identical. One very frequently meets with the statement that the teachings of socialism are nothing more or less than the teachings of Christianity. This contention is discussed in the following pages, where the conclusion will be reached that, far from being in agreement, socialism and Christian economics contradict each other on many fundamental points. It is, however, not the aim of the discussion to appraise the relative merits of either system, or to applaud one and disparage the other. All that it is sought to do is to distinguish between them ; and to demonstrate that, whatever be the merits or demerits of the two philosophies, they are two, and not one.

SECTION 4.—DIVISION OF THE SUBJECT

The opinion is general that the distinctive doctrine of the mediæval Church which permeated the whole of its economic thought was the doctrine of usury. The holders of this view may lay claim to very influential supporters among the students of the subject. Ashley says that ' the prohibition of usury was clearly the centre

of the canonist doctrine.'[1] Roscher expresses
the same opinion in practically the same words;[2]
and Endemann sees the whole economic development of the Middle Ages and the Renaissance as
the victorious destruction of the usury law by the
exigencies of real life.[3] However impressed we
may be by the opinions of such eminent authorities, we, nevertheless, cannot help feeling that on
this point they are under a misconception. There
is no doubt that the doctrine of the canonists
which impresses the modern mind most deeply
is the usury prohibition, partly because it is not
generally realised that the usury doctrine would
not have forbidden the receipt of any of the
commonest kinds of unearned revenue of the
present day, and partly because the discussion of
usury occupies such a very large part of the
writings of the canonists. It may be quite true
to say that the doctrine of usury was that which
gave the greatest trouble to the mediæval writers,
on account of the nicety of the distinctions with
which it abounded, and on account of the ingenuity
of avaricious merchants, who continually sought
to evade the usury laws by disguising illegal under
the guise of legal transactions. In practice, therefore, the usury doctrine was undoubtedly the
most prominent part of the canonist teaching,

[1] *Op. cit.*, vol. i. pt. ii. p. 399.
[2] ' Bekanntlich war das Wucherverbot der praktische Mittelpunkt der
ganzen kanonischen Wirthschaftspolitik,' *op. cit.*, p. 8.
[3] *Studien,* vol. i. p. 2 and *passim*. At vol. ii. p. 31 it is stated that
the teaching on just price is a corollary of the usury teaching. But
Aquinas treats of usury in the article *following* his treatment of just
price.

because it was the part which most tempted evasion; but to admit that is not to agree with the proposition that it was the centre of the canonist doctrine. Our view is that the teaching on usury was simply one of the applications of the doctrine that all voluntary exchanges of property must be regulated by the precepts of commutative justice. In one sense it might be said to be a corollary of the doctrine of just price. This is apparently the suggestion of Dr. Cleary in his excellent book on usury : ' It seems to me that the so-called loan of money is really a sale, and that a loan of meal, wine, oil, gunpowder, and similar commodities— that is to say, commodities which are consumed in use—is also a sale. If this is so, as I believe it is, then loans of all these consumptible goods should be regulated by the principles which regulate sale contracts. A just price only may be taken, and the return must be truly equivalent.' [1] This statement of Dr. Cleary's seems well warranted, and finds support in the analogy which was drawn between the legitimacy of interest—in the technical sense—and the legitimacy of a vendor's increasing the price of an article by reason of some special inconvenience which he would suffer by parting with it. Both these titles were justified on the same ground, namely, that they were in the nature of compensations, and arose independently of the main contract of loan or sale as the case might be. ' Le vendeur est en présence de l'acheteur. L'objet a pour

[1] *The Church and Usury*, p. 186.

lui une valeur particulière : c'est un souvenir,
par exemple. A-t-il le droit de majorer le prix
de vente ? de dépasser le juste prix convenu ?
. . . Avec l'unanimité des docteurs on peut
trouver légitime la majoration du prix. L'évalu-
ation commune distingue un double élément dans
l'objet : sa valeur ordinaire à laquelle répond le
juste prix, et cette valeur extraordinaire qui
appartient au vendeur, dont il se prive et qui
mérite une compensation : il le fait pour ainsi
dire l'objet d'un second contrat qui se superpose
au premier. Cela est si vrai que le supplément de
prix n'est pas dû au même titre que le juste prix.' [1]
The importance of this analogy will appear when
we come to treat just price and usury in detail ;
it is simply referred to here in support of the
proposition that, far from being a special doctrine
sui generis, the usury doctrine of the Church was
simply an application to the sale of consumptible
things of the universal rules which applied to all
sales. In other words, the doctrines of the just
price and of usury were founded on the same
fundamental precept of justice in exchange. If
we indicate what this precept was, we can claim
to have indicated what was the true centre of
the canonist doctrine.

The scholastic teaching on the subject of the
rules of justice in exchange was founded on the
famous fifth book of Aristotle's *Ethics*, and is
very clearly set forth by Aquinas. In the article
of the *Summa*, where the question is discussed,

---

[1] Desbuquois, 'La Justice dans l'Echange,' *Semaine Sociale de France*,
1911, p. 174.

' Whether the mean is to be observed in the same
way in distributive as in commutative justice ? '
we find a clear exposition : ' In commutations
something is delivered to an individual on account
of something of his that has been received, as may
be seen chiefly in selling and buying, where the
notion of commutation is found primarily. Hence
it is necessary to equalise thing with thing, so that
the one person should pay back to the other just
so much as he has become richer out of that which
belonged to the other. The result of this will be
equality according to the *arithmetical* mean, which
is gauged according to equal excess in quantity.
Thus 5 is the mean between 6 and 4, since it
exceeds the latter, and is exceeded by the former
by 1. Accordingly, if at the start both persons
have 5, and one of them receives 1 out of the
other's belongings, the one that is the receiver
will have 6, and the other will be left with 4 : and
so there will be justice if both are brought back
to the mean, 1 being taken from him that has 6
and given to him that has 4, for then both will
have 5, which is the mean.' [1] In the following
article the matter of each kind of justice is discussed. We are told that : ' Justice is about
certain external operations, namely, distribution
and commutation. These consist in the use of
certain externals, whether things, persons, or
even works : of things as when one man takes
from or restores to another that which is his : of
persons as when a man does an injury to the very
person of another . . . : and of works as when

[1] II. ii. 61, 2.

a man justly enacts a work of another or does a
work for him. . . . Commutative justice directs
commutations that can take place between two
persons. Of these some are involuntary, some
voluntary. . . . Voluntary commutations are
when a man voluntarily transfers his chattel to
another person. And if he transfer it simply so
that the recipient incurs no debt, as in the case
of gifts, it is an act not of justice, but of liberality.
A voluntary transfer belongs to justice in so far
as it includes the notion of debt.' Aquinas then
goes on to distinguish between the different kinds
of contract, sale, usufruct, loan, letting and hiring,
and deposit, and concludes, ' In all these actions
the mean is taken in the same way according
to the equality of repayment. Hence all these
actions belong to the one species of justice, namely,
commutative justice.' [1]

This is not the place to discuss the precise
meaning of the equality upon which Aquinas
insists, which will be more properly considered
when we come to deal with the just price. What
is to be noticed at present is that all the transactions which are properly comprised in a discussion
of economic theory—sales, loans, etc.—are grouped
together as being subject to the same regulative
principle. It therefore appears more correct to approach the subject which we are attempting to treat
by following that principle into its various applications, than by making one particular application of
the principle the starting-point of the discussion.

[1] II. ii. 61, 3. The reasoning of Aristotle is characteristically rein-
forced by the quotation of Matt. vii. 12 ; II. ii. 77, 1.

It will be noticed, however, that the principles of
commutative justice all treat of the commutations
of external goods—in other words, they assume the
existence of property of external goods in individuals. Commutations are but a result of private
property ; in a state of communism there could be
no commutation. This is well pointed out by Gerson [1] and by Nider.[2] It consequently is important,
before discussing exchange of ownership, to discuss
the principle of ownership itself ; or, in other words,
to study the static before the dynamic state.[3]

We shall therefore deal in the first place with
the right of private property, which we shall show
to have been fully recognised by the mediæval
writers. We shall then point out the duties
which this right entailed, and shall establish the
position that the scholastic teaching was directed
equally against modern socialistic principles and
modern unregulated individualism. The next
point with which we shall deal is the exchange of
property between individuals, which is a necessary corollary of the right of property. We shall
show that such exchanges were regulated by well-
defined principles of commutative justice, which
applied equally in the case of the sale of goods
and in the case of the sale of the use of money.
The last matter with which we shall deal is the

---

[1] *De Contractibus,* i. 4 : ' Inventa est autem commutatio civilis post
peccatum quoniam status innocentiæ habuit omnia communia.'

[2] *De Contractibus,* v. 1 : ' Nunc videndum est breviter unde originaliter
proveniat quod rerum dominia sunt distincta, sic quod hoc dicatur
meum et illud tuum ; quia illud est fundamentum omnis injustitiae
in contractando rem alienam, et post omnis injustitia reddendo eam.'

[3] See l'Abbé Desbuquois, *op. cit.*, p. 168.

machinery by which exchanges are conducted, namely, money. Many other subjects, such as slavery and the legitimacy of commerce, will be treated as they arise in the course of our treatment of these principal divisions.

In its ultimate analysis, the whole subject may be reduced to a classification of the various duties which attached to the right of private property. The owner of property, as we shall see, was bound to observe certain duties in respect of its acquisition and its consumption, and certain other duties in respect of its exchange, whether it consisted of goods or of money. The whole fabric of mediæval economics was based on the foundation of private property; and the elaborate and logical system of regulations to ensure justice in economic life would have had no purpose or no use if the subject matter of that justice were abolished.

It must not be understood that the mediæval writers treated economic subjects in this order, or in any order at all. As we have already said, economic matters are simply referred to in connection with ethics, and were not detached and treated as making up a distinct body of teaching. Ashley says : ' The reader will guard himself against supposing that any mediæval writer ever detached these ideas from the body of his teaching, and put them together as a modern text-book writer might do ; or that they were ever presented in this particular order, and with the connecting argument definitely stated.' [1]

[1] Op. cit., vol. i. pt. ii. p. 387.

CHAPTER II

PROPERTY

Section 1.—The Right to Procure and Dispense Property

The teaching of the mediæval Church on the subject of property was perfectly simple and clear. Aquinas devoted a section of the *Summa* to it, and his opinion was accepted as final by all the later writers of the period, who usually repeat his very words. However, before coming to quote and explain Aquinas, it is necessary to deal with a difficulty that has occurred to several students of Christian economics, namely, that the teaching of the scholastics on the subject of property was in some way opposed to the teaching of the early Church and of Christ Himself. Thus Haney says : ' It is necessary to keep the ideas of Christianity and the Church separate, for few will deny that Christianity as a religion is quite distinct from the various institutions or Churches which profess it. . . .' And he goes on to point out that, whereas Christianity recommended community of property, the Church permitted private property and inequality.[1] Strictly speaking, the reconciliation of the mediæval teaching with that

[1] *Op. cit.*, p. 73.

of the primitive Church might be said to be outside the scope of the present essay. In our opinion, however, it is important to insist upon the fundamental harmony of the teaching of the Church in the two periods, in the first place, because it is impossible to understand the later without an understanding of the earlier doctrine from which it developed, and secondly, because of the widespread prevalence, even among Catholics, of the erroneous idea that the scholastic teaching was opposed to the ethical principle laid down by the Founder of Christianity.

Amongst the arguments which are advanced by socialists none is more often met than the alleged socialist teaching and practice of the early Christians. For instance, Cabet's *Voyage en Icarie* contains the following passage : ' Mais quand on s'enfonce sérieusement et ardemment dans la question de savoir comment la société pourrait être organisée en Démocratie, c'est-à-dire sur les bases de l'Egalité et de la Fraternité, on arrive à reconnaître que cette organisation exige et entraîne nécessairement la communauté de biens. Et nous hâtons d'ajouter que cette communauté était également proclamée par Jésus-Christ, par tous ses apôtres et ses disciples, par tous les pères de l'Église et tous les Chrétiens des premiers siècles.' The fact that St. Thomas Aquinas, the great exponent of Catholic teaching in the Middle Ages, defends in unambiguous language the institution of private property offers no difficulties to the socialist historian of Christianity. He replies simply that St. Thomas wrote

in an age when the Church was the Church of the
rich as well as of the poor ; that it had to modify
its doctrines to ease the consciences of its rich
members ; and that, ever since the conversion of
Constantine, the primitive Christian teaching on
property had been progressively corrupted by
motives of expediency, until the time of the
Summa, when it had ceased to resemble in any way
the teaching of the Apostles.[1] We must therefore
first of all demonstrate that there is no such contradiction between the teaching of the Apostles
and that of the mediæval Church on the subject
of private property, but that, on the contrary,
the necessity of private property was at all times
recognised and insisted on by the Catholic Church.
As it is put in an anonymous article in the *Dublin
Review* : ' Among Christian nations we discover
at a very early period a strong tendency towards
a general and equitable distribution of wealth
and property among the whole body politic.
Grounded on an ever-increasing historical evidence, we might possibly affirm that the mediæval
Church brought her whole weight to bear inces-
santly upon this one singular and single point.' [2]

The alleged communism of the first Christians

[1] See, *e.g.,* Nitti, *Catholic Socialism,* p. 71. ' Thus, then, according
to Nitti, the Christian Church has been guilty of the meanest, most
selfish, and most corrupt utilitarianism in her attitude towards the
question of wealth and property. She was communistic when she
had nothing. She blessed poverty in order to fill her own coffers.
And when the coffers were full she took rank among the owners of land
and houses, she became zealous in the interests of property, and proclaimed that its origin was divine ' (' The Fathers of the Church and
Socialism,' by Dr. Hogan, *Irish Ecclesiastical Record,* vol. xxv. p. 226).

[2] ' Christian Political Economy,' *Dublin Review,* N.S., vol. vi. p. 356.

is based on a few verses of the Acts of the Apostles describing the condition of the Church of Jerusalem. ' And they that believed were together and had all things common ; And sold their possessions and goods, and parted them to all men, as every man had need.' [1] ' And the multitude of them that believed were of one heart and of one soul : neither said any of them that aught of the things which he possessed was his own ; but they had all things common. Neither was there any amongst them that lacked : for as many as were possessors of land or houses sold them, and brought the price of the things that were sold, And laid them down at the apostles' feet : and distribution was made unto every man according as he had need.' [2]

It is by no means clear whether the state of things here depicted really amounted to communism in the strict sense. Several of the most enlightened students of the Bible have come to the conclusion that the verses quoted simply express in a striking way the great liberality and benevolence which prevailed among the Christian fraternity at Jerusalem. This view was strongly asserted by Mosheim,[3] and is held by Dr. Carlyle. ' A more careful examination of the passages in the Acts,' says the latter,[4] ' show clearly enough that this was no systematic division of property, but that the charitable instinct of the infant

---

[1] ii. 44-45.   [2] iv. 32, 34, 35.

[3] *Dissert. ad Hist. Eccles.*, vol. ii. p. 1.

[4] ' The Political Theory of the Ante-Nicene Fathers,' *Economic Review*, vol. ix.

Church was so great that those who were in want were completely supported by those who were more prosperous. . . . Still there was no systematic communism, no theory of the necessity of it.' Colour is lent to this interpretation by the fact that similar words and phrases were used to emphasise the prevalence of charity and benevolence in later communities of Christians, amongst whom, as we know from other sources, the right of private property was fully admitted. Thus Tertullian wrote : [1] ' One in mind and soul, we do not hesitate to share our earthly goods with one another. All things are common among us but our wives.' This passage, if it were taken alone, would be quite as strong and unambiguous as those from the Acts ; but fortunately, a few lines higher up, Tertullian had described how the Church was supported, wherein he showed most clearly that private property was still recognised and practised : ' Though we have our treasure-chest, it is not made up of purchase-money, as of a religion that has its price. On the monthly collection day, if he likes, each puts in a small donation ; but only if he has pleasure, and only if he be able ; all is voluntary.' This point is well put by Bergier : [2] ' Towards the end of the first century St. Barnabas ; in the second, St. Justin and St. Lucian ; in the third, St. Clement of Alexandria, Tertullian, Origen, St. Cyprian ; in the fourth, Arnobius and Lactantius, say that among the Christians all goods are common ;

[1] *Apol.* 39.
[2] *Dictionnaire de Théologie*, Paris, 1829, tit. ' Communauté.'

there was then certainly no question of a communism of goods taken in the strict sense.' It is therefore doubtful if the Church at Jerusalem, as described in the Acts, practised communism at all, as apart from great liberality and benevolence. Assuming, however, that the Acts should be interpreted in their strict literal sense, let us see to what the so-called communism amounted. In the first place, it is plain from Acts iv. 32 that the communism was one of use, not of ownership. It was not until the individual owner had sold his goods and placed the proceeds in the common fund that any question of communism arose. ' Whiles it remained was it not thine own,' said St. Peter, rebuking Ananias, ' and after it was sold was it not in thine own power ? ' [1] This distinction is particularly important in view of the fact that it is precisely that insisted on by St. Thomas Aquinas. There is no reason to suppose that the community of use practised at Jerusalem was in any way different from that advocated by Aquinas—namely, ' the possession by a man of external things, not as his own, but in common, so that, to wit, he is ready to communicate them to others in their need.'

In the next place, we must observe that the communism described in the Acts was purely voluntary. This is quite obvious from the relation in the fifth chapter of the incident of Ananias and Sapphira. There is no indication that the abandonment of one's possessory rights was

[1] Roscher, *Political Economy* (Eng. trans.), vol. i. p. 246 ; *Catholic Encyclopædia*, tit. ' Communism.'

preached by the Apostles. Indeed, it would be
difficult to understand why they should have
done so, when Christ Himself had remained silent
on the subject.   Far from advocating communism,
the Founder of Christianity had urged the practice
of many virtues for which the possession of private
property was essential. ' What Christ recommended,' says Sudre,[1] ' was voluntary abnegation
or alms-giving. But the giving of goods without
any hope of compensation, the spontaneous de-
privation of oneself, could not exist except under
a system of private property . . . they were one
of the ways of exercising such rights.' Moreover,
as the same author points out, private property
was fully recognised under the Jewish dispensa-
tion, and Christ would therefore have made use of
explicit language if he had intended to alter the
old law in this fundamental respect. ' Think not
that I am come to destroy the law or the prophets :
I am not come to destroy, but to fulfil.' [2]   At the
time of Christ's preaching, a Jewish sect, the
Essenes, were endeavouring to put into practice
the ideals of communism, but there is not a word in
the Gospels to suggest that He ever held them up as
an example to His followers. ' Communism was
never preached by Christ, although it was practised
under His very eyes by the Essenes. This absolute
silence is equivalent to an implicit condemnation.'[3]

[1] *Histoire du Communisme*, p. 39.   [2] Matt. v. 17.
[3] Sudre, *op. cit.*, p. 44. On the Essenes see ' Historic Phases of
Socialism,' by Dr. Hogan, *Irish Ecclesiastical Record*, vol. xxv. p. 334.
Even Huet discounts the importance of this instance of communism,
Le Règne social du Christianisme, p. 38.

Nor was communism preached as part of Christ's doctrine as taught by the Apostles. In Paul's epistles there is no direction to the congregations addressed that they should abandon their private property ; on the contrary, the continued existence of such rights is expressly recognised and approved in his appeals for funds for the Church at Jerusalem.[1] Can it be that, as Roscher says,[2] the experiment in communism had produced a chronic state of poverty in the Church at Jerusalem ? Certain it is the experiment was never repeated in any of the other apostolic congregations. The communism at Jerusalem, if it ever existed at all, not only failed to spread to other Churches, but failed to continue at Jerusalem itself. It is universally admitted by competent students of the question that the phenomenon was but temporary and transitory.[3]

The utterances of the Fathers of the Church on property are scattered and disconnected. Nevertheless, there is sufficient cohesion in them to enable us to form an opinion of their teaching on the subject. It has, as we have said, frequently been asserted that they favoured a system of communism, and disapproved of private ownership. The supporters of this view base their arguments on a number of isolated texts, taken out of their context, and not interpreted with any regard to the circumstances in which they were written.

[1] e.g. Rom. xv. 26, 1 Cor. xvi. 1.
[2] Political Economy, vol. i. p. 246.
[3] Sudre, op. cit. ; Salvador, Jésus-Christ et sa Doctrine, vol. ii. p. 221. See More's Utopia.

'The mistake,' as Devas says,[1] 'of representing
the early Christian Fathers of the Church as rank
socialists is frequently made by those who are
friendly to modern socialism; the reason for it
is that either they have taken passages of orthodox writers apart from their context, and without
due regard to the circumstances in which they
were written, and the meaning they would have
conveyed to their hearers; or else, by a grosser
blunder, the perversions of heretics are set forth
as the doctrine of the Church, and a sad case
arises of mistaken identity.' A careful study of
the patristic texts bearing on the subject leads one
to the conclusion that Mr. Devas's view is without
doubt the correct one.[2]

The passages from the writings of the Fathers
which are cited by socialists who are anxious to
support the proposition that socialism formed
part of the early Christian teaching may be
roughly divided into four groups : first, passages
where the abandonment of earthly possessions is

[1] *Dublin Review*, Jan. 1898.

[2] Dr. Hogan, in an article entitled ' The Fathers of the Church and
Socialism,' in the *Irish Ecclesiastical Record*, vol. xxv. p. 226, has
examined all the texts relative to property in the writings of Tertullian,
St. Justin Martyn, St. Clement of Rome, St. Clement of Alexandria,
St. Basil, St. Ambrose, St. John Chrysostom, St. Augustine, and St.
Gregory the Great; and the utterances of St. Basil, St. Ambrose, and St.
Jerome are similarly examined in ' The Alleged Socialism of the Church
Fathers,' by Dr. John A. Ryan. The patristic texts are also fully
examined by Abbé Calippe in ' Le Caractère sociale de la Propriété '
in *La Semaine Sociale de France*, 1909, p. 111. The conclusion come
to after thorough examinations such as these is always the same. For
a good analysis of the patristic texts from the communistic standpoint,
see Conrad Noel, *Socialism in Church History*.

held up as a work of more than ordinary devotion
—in other words, a counsel of perfection ; second,
those where the practice of almsgiving is recommended in the rhetorical and persuasive language
of the missioner—where the faithful are exhorted
to exercise their charity to such a degree that it
may be said that the rich and the poor have
all things in common ; third, passages directed
against avarice and the wrongful acquisition or
abuse of riches ; and fourth, passages where the
distinction between the natural and positive law
on the matter is explained.

The following passage from Cyprian is a good
example of an utterance which was clearly meant
as a counsel of perfection. Isolated sentences
from this passage have frequently been quoted to
prove that Cyprian was an advocate of communism ; but there can be no doubt from the
passage as a whole, that all that he was aiming at
was to cultivate in his followers a high detachment from earthly wealth, and that, in so far as
complete abandonment of one's property is recommended, it is simply indicated as a work of
quite unusual devotion. It is noteworthy that
this passage occurs in a treatise on almsgiving, a
practice which presupposes a system of individual
ownership : [1] 'Let us consider what the congre-
gation of believers did in the time of the Apostles,
when at the first beginnings the mind flourished
with greater virtues, when the faith of believers
burned with a warmth of faith yet new. Thus
they sold houses and farms, and gladly and liber-

[1] *De Opere et Eleemosynis,* 25.

ally presented to the Apostles the proceeds to be
dispersed to the poor ; selling and alienating their
earthly estate, they transferred their lands thither
where they might receive the fruits of an eternal
possession, and there prepared houses where they
might begin an eternal habitation. Such, then, was
the abundance in labours as was the agreement in
love, as we read in the Acts—" Neither said any of
them that aught of the things which he possessed
was his own ; but they had all things common."
This is truly to become son of God by spiritual
birth ; this is to imitate by the heavenly law the
equity of God the Father. For whatever is of
God is common in our use ; nor is any one excluded
from His benefits and His gifts so as to prevent the
whole human race from enjoying equally the
divine goodness and liberality. Thus the day
equally enlightens, the sun gives radiance, the rain
moistens, the wind blows, and the sleep is one to
those who sleep, and the splendour of Stars and
of the Moon is common. In which examples of
equality he who as a possessor in the earth shares
his returns and his fruits with the fraternity, while
he is common and just in his gratuitous bounties,
is an imitator of God the Father.'

There is a much-quoted passage of St. John
Chrysostom which is capable of the same interpretation. In his commentary on the alleged
communistic existence of the Apostles at Jerusalem
the Saint emphasises the fact that their communism was voluntary : ' That this was in consequence not merely of the miraculous signs, but
of their own purpose, is manifest from the case of

Ananias and Sapphira.' He further insists on the fact that the members of this community were animated by unusual fervour : ' From the exceeding ardour of the givers none was in want.' Further down, in the same homily, St. John Chrysostom urges the adoption of a communistic system of housekeeping, but purely on the grounds of domestic economy and saving of labour. There is not a word to suggest that a communistic system was morally preferable to a proprietary one.[1]

The second class of patristic texts which are relied on by socialists are, as we have said, those ' where the practice of almsgiving is recommended in the rhetorical and persuasive language of the missioner—where the faithful are exhorted to exercise their charity to such a degree that it may be said that the rich and poor have all things in common.' Such passages are very frequent throughout the writings of the Fathers, but we may give as examples two, which are most frequently relied on by socialists. One of these is from St. Ambrose : [2] ' Mercy is a part of justice ; and if you wish to give to the poor, this mercy is justice. " He hath dispersed, he hath given to the poor ; his righteousness endureth for ever." [3] It is therefore unjust that one should not be helped by his neighbour ; when God hath wished

---

[1] *Hom. on Acts* xi. That voluntary poverty was regarded as a counsel of perfection by Aquinas is abundantly clear from many passages in his works, *e.g. Summa,* I. ii. 108, 4 ; II. ii. 185, 6 ; II. ii. 186, 3 ; *Summa cont. Gent.,* iii. 133. On this, as on every other point, the teaching of Aquinas is in line with that of the Fathers.

[2] *Comm. on Ps. cxviii.,* viii. 22.   [3] Ps. cxii. 9.

the possession of the earth to be common to all
men, and its fruits to minister to all ; but avarice
established possessory rights. It is therefore
just that if you lay claim to anything as your
private property, which is really conferred in
common to the whole human race, that you should
dispense something to the poor, so that you may
not deny nourishment to those who have the right
to share with you.' The following passage from
Gregory the Great [1] is another example of this
kind of passage : ' Those who rather desire what
is another's, nor bestow that is their own, are to
be admonished to consider carefully that the
earth out of which they are taken is common to
all men, and therefore brings forth nourishment
for all in common. Vainly, then, do they suppose
themselves innocent who claim to their own
private use the common gift of God ; those who
in not imparting what they have received walk in
the midst of the slaughter of their neighbours ;
since they almost daily slay so many persons as
there are dying poor whose subsidies they keep
close in their own possession.'

The third class of passages to which reference
must be made is composed of the numerous
attacks which the Fathers levelled against the
abuse or wrongful acquisition of riches. These
passages do not indicate that the Fathers favoured
a system of communism, but point in precisely
the contrary direction. If property were an evil
thing in itself, they would not have wasted so
much time in emphasising the evil uses to which

[1] *Lib. Reg. Past.*, iii. 21.

it was sometimes put. The insistence on the abuses of an institution is an implicit admission that it has its uses. Thus Clement of Alexandria devotes a whole treatise to answering the question ' Who is the rich man who can be saved ? ' in which it appears quite plainly that it is the possible abuse of wealth, and the possible too great attachment to worldly goods, that are the principal dangers in the way of a rich man's salvation. The suggestion that in order to be saved a man must abandon all his property is strongly controverted. The following passage from St. Gregory Nazianzen [1] breathes the same spirit : ' One of us has oppressed the poor, and wrested from him his portion of land, and wrongly encroached upon his landmarks by fraud or violence, and joined house to house, and field to field, to rob his neighbour of something, and has been eager to have no neighbour, so as to dwell alone on the earth. Another has defiled the land with usury and interest, both gathering where he has not sowed and reaping where he has not strewn, farming not the land but the necessity of the needy. . . . Another has had no pity on the widow and orphans, and not imparted his bread and meagre nourishment to the needy ; . . . a man perhaps of much property unexpectedly gained, for this is the most unjust of all, who finds his very barns too narrow for him, filling some and emptying others to build greater ones for future crops.' Similarly Clement of Rome advo- cates *frugality* in the enjoyment of wealth ; [2] and

[1] *Orat.*, xvi. 18.   [2] *The Instructor*, iii. 7.

Salvian has a long passage on the dangers of the abuse of riches.[1]

The fourth group of passages is that in which the distinction between the natural and positive law on the matter is explained. It is here that the greatest confusion has been created by socialist writers, who conclude, because they read in the works of some of the Fathers that private property did not exist by natural law, that it was therefore condemned by them as an illegitimate institution. Nothing could be more erroneous. All that the Fathers meant in these passages was that in the state of nature—the idealised Golden Age of the pagans, or the Garden of Eden of the Christians—there was no individual ownership of goods. The very moment, however, that man fell from that ideal state, communism became impossible, simply on account of the change that had taken place in man's own nature. To this extent it is true to say that the Fathers regarded property with disapproval; it was one of the institutions rendered necessary by the fall of man. Of course it would have been preferable that man should not have fallen from his natural innocence, in which case he could have lived a life of communism; but, as he had fallen, and communism had from that moment become impossible, property must be respected as the one institution which could put a curb on his avarice, and preserve a society of fallen men from chaos and general rapine.

That this is the correct interpretation of the patristic utterances regarding property and natural

[1] *Ad Eccles.*, i. 7.

law appears from the following passage of *The Divine Institution* of Lactantius—'the most explicit statement bearing on the Christian idea of property in the first four centuries' :[1] ' "They preferred to live content with a simple mode of life," as Cicero relates in his poems ; and this is peculiar to our religion. "It was not even allowed to mark out or to divide the plain with a boundary : men sought all things in common,"[2] since God had given the earth in common to all, that they might pass their life in common, not that mad and raging avarice might claim all things for itself, and that riches produced for all might not be wanting to any. And this saying of the poet ought so to be taken, not as suggesting the idea that individuals at that time had no private property, but it must be regarded as a poetical figure, that we may understand that men were so liberal, that they did not shut up the fruits of the earth produced for them, nor did they in solitude brood over the things stored up, but admitted the poor to share the fruits of their labour :

"Now streams of milk, now streams of nectar flowed."[3]

And no wonder, since the storehouses of the good literally lay open to all. Nor did avarice intercept the divine bounty, and thus cause hunger and thirst in common ; but all alike had abundance, since they who had possessions gave liberally and bountifully to those who had not. But after Saturnus had been banished from heaven, and

---

[1] 'The Biblical and Early Christian Idea of Property,' by Dr. V. Bartlett, in *Property, its Duties and Rights* (London, 1913).

[2] *Georg.*, i. 126.   [3] Ovid, *Met.*, I. iii.

had arrived in Latium . . . not only did the people who had a superfluity fail to bestow a share upon others, but they even seized the property of others, drawing everything to their private gain; and the things which formerly even individuals laboured to obtain for the common use of all were now conveyed to the powers of a few. For that they might subdue others by slavery, they began to withdraw and collect together the necessaries of life, and to keep them firmly shut up, that they might make the bounties of heaven their own; not on account of kindness (*humanitas*), a feeling which had no existence for them, but that they might sweep together all the instruments of lust and avarice.' [1]

It appears from the above passage that Lactantius regarded the era in which a system of communism existed as long since vanished, if indeed it ever had existed. The same idea emerges from the writings of St. Augustine, who drew a distinction between divine and human right. ' By what right does every man possess what he possesses ? ' he asks.[2] ' Is it not by human right ? For by divine right "the earth is the Lord's, and the fullness thereof." The poor and the rich God made of one clay; the same earth supports alike the poor and the rich. By human right, however, one says, This estate is mine, this servant is mine, this house is mine. By human right, therefore, is by right of the Emperor. Why so ? Because God has distributed to mankind these very human

---

[1] Lactantius, *Div. Inst.*, v. 5-6.
[2] *Tract in Joh. Ev.*, vi. 25.

rights through the emperors and kings of the
world.'

The socialist commentators of St. Augustine
have strained this, and similar passages, to mean
that because property rests on human, and not
on divine, right, therefore it should not exist
at all. It is, of course true that what human
right has created human right can repeal ; and
it is therefore quite fair to argue that all the
citizens of a community might agree to live a life
of communism. That is simply an argument to
prove that there is nothing immoral in communism,
and does not prove in the very slightest degree
that there is anything immoral in property. On
the contrary, so long as ' the emperors and kings
of the world ' ordain that private property shall
continue, it would be, according to St. Augustine,
immoral for any individual to maintain that such
ordinances were wrongful.

The correct meaning of the patristic distinction
between natural and positiv) law with regard to
property is excellently summarised in Dr. Carlyle's
essay on *Property in Mediæval Theology* : [1] ' What
do the expressions of the Fathers mean ? At
first sight they might seem to be an assertion of
communism, or denunciation of private property
as a thing which is sinful or unlawful. But this
is not what the Fathers mean. There can be
little doubt that we find the sources of these words
in such a phrase as that of Cicero—" Sunt autem
privata nulla natura " [2]—and in the Stoic tradition

---

[1] *Property, Its Duties and Rights* (London, 1913).
[2] *De Off.*, i. 7.

which is represented in one of Seneca's letters, when he describes the primitive life in which men lived together in peace and happiness, when there was no system of coercive government and no private property, and says that man passed out of this primitive condition as their first innocence disappeared, as they became avaricious and dissatisfied with the common enjoyment of the good things of the world, and desired to hold them as their private possession.[1] Here we have the quasi-philosophical theory, from which the patristic conception is derived. When men were innocent there was no need for private property, or the other great conventional institutions of society, but as this innocence passed away, they found themselves compelled to organise society and to devise institutions which should regulate the ownership and use of the good things which men had once held in common. The institution of property thus represents the fall of man from his primitive innocence, through greed and avarice, which refused to recognise the common ownership of things, and also the method by which the blind greed of human nature might be controlled and regulated. It is this ambiguous origin of the institution which explains how the Fathers could hold that private property was not natural, that it grew out of men's vicious and sinful desires, and at the same time that it was a legitimate institution.'

Janet takes the same view of the patristic utterances on this subject: [2] 'What do the Fathers

[1] Seneca, *Ep.*, xiv. 2.
[2] *Histoire de la Science politique*, vol. i. p. 330.

say ? It is that in Jesus Christ there is no mine
and thine.   Nothing is more true, without doubt;
in the divine order, in the order of absolute
charity, where men are wholly wrapt up in God,
distinction and inequality of goods would be impossible. But the Fathers saw clearly that such
a state of things was not realisable here below.
What did they do ?   They established property on
human law, positive law, imperial law.   Communism is either a Utopia or a barbarism ; a Utopia
if one imagine it founded on universal devotion ;
a barbarism if one imposes it by force.' [1]

It must not be concluded that the evidence of
the approbation by the Fathers of private property
is purely negative or solely derived from the
interpretation of possibly ambiguous texts.   On
the contrary, the lawfulness of property is emphatically asserted on more than one occasion.
' To possess riches,' says Hilary of Poictiers,[2] ' is
not wrongful, but rather the manner in which
possession is used. . . . It is a crime to possess
wrongfully rather than simply to possess.'   ' Who
does not understand,' asks St. Augustine,[3] ' that
it is not sinful to possess riches, but to love
and place hope in them, and to prefer them to
truth or justice ? '   Again, ' Why do you reproach
us by saying that men renewed in baptism ought
no longer to beget children or to possess fields and
houses and money ?   Paul allows it.' [4]   According
to Ambrose,[5] ' Riches themselves are not wrong-

---

[1] See also Jarrett, *Mediæval Socialism*.
[2] *Comm. on Matt. xix.* 9.   [3] *Contra Ad.*, xx. 2.
[4] *De Mor. Eccl. Cath.*, i. 35.   [5] *Epist.*, lxiii. 92.

ful. Indeed, "redemptio animæ viri divitiæ
ejus," because he who gives to the poor saves his
soul. There is therefore a place for goodness in
these material riches. You are as steersmen in
a great sea. He who steers his ship well, quickly
crosses the waves, and comes to port ; but he who
does not know how to control his ship is sunk by
his own weight. Wherefore it is written, "Pos-
sessio divitum civitas firmissima." ' A Council
in A.D. 415 condemned the proposition held by
Pelagius that ' the rich cannot be saved unless
they renounced their goods.' [1]

The more one studies the Fathers the more one
becomes convinced that property was regarded
by them as one of the normal and legitimate
institutions of human society. Benigni's conclusion, as the result of his exceptionally thorough
researches, is that according to the early Fathers,
' property is lawful and ought scrupulously to be
respected. But property is subject to the high
duties of human fellowship which sprang from the
equality and brotherhood of man. Collectivism
is absurd and immoral.' [2] Janet arrived at the
same conclusion : ' In spite of the words of the
Fathers, in spite of the advice given by Christ
to the rich man to sell all his goods and give to the
poor, in spite of the communism of the Apostles,
can one say that Christianity condemned property ?
Certainly not. Christianity considered it a counsel of perfection for a man to deprive himself of
his goods ; it did not abrogate the right of any-

---

[1] *Revue Archéologique*, 1880, p. 321.
[2] *L'Economia Sociale Christiana avanti Costantino* (Genoa, 1897).

body.'[1] The same conclusion is reached by the
Abbé Calippe in an excellent article published in
La Semaine Sociale de France, 1909. 'The right of
property and of the property owner are assumed.'[2]
'It is only prejudiced or superficial minds which
could make the writers of the fourth century the
precursors of modern communists or collectivists.'[3]
When we turn to St. Thomas Aquinas, we find
that his teaching on the subject of property is not at
all out of harmony with that of the earlier Fathers
of the Church, but, on the contrary, summarises
and consolidates it. 'It remained to elaborate,
to constitute a definite theory of the right of property. It sufficed to harmonise, to collaborate,
and to relate one to the other these elements
furnished by the Christian doctors of the first four
or five centuries ; and this was precisely the work
of the great theologians of the Middle Ages,
especially of St. Thomas Aquinas. . . . In estab-
lishing his thesis St. Thomas did not borrow
from the Roman jurisconsults through the medium
of St. Isidore more than their vocabulary, their
formulas, their juridical distinctions ; he also
borrowed from Aristotle the arguments upon
which the philosopher based his right of property.
But the ground of his doctrine is undoubtedly of
Christian origin. There is, between the Fathers
and him, a perfect continuity.'[4] 'Community
of goods,' he writes, 'is ascribed to the natural
law, not that the natural law dictates that all

---

[1] *Histoire de la Science politique*, vol. i. p. 319.
[2] P. 114.   [3] P. 121.
[4] Abbé Calippe, *op. cit.*, 1909, p. 124.

things should be possessed in common, and that nothing should be possessed as one's own ; but because the division of possession is not according to the natural law, but rather arose from human agreement, which belongs to positive law. Hence the ownership of possessions is not contrary to the natural law, but an addition thereto devised by human reason.' This is simply another way of stating St. Augustine's distinction between natural and positive law. If it speaks with more respect of positive law than St. Augustine had done, it is because Aquinas was influenced by the Aristotelian conception of the State being itself a natural institution, owing to man being a social animal.[1]

The explanation which St. Thomas gives of the necessity for property also shows how clearly he agreed with the Fathers' teaching on natural communism : ' Two things are competent to man in respect of external things. One is the power to procure and dispense them, and in this regard it is lawful for a man to possess property. Moreover, this is necessary to human life for three reasons. First, because every man is more careful to procure what is for himself alone than that which is common to many or to all : since each one would shirk the labour, and would leave to another that which concerns the community, as happens when there is a great number of servants.

[1] See Carlyle, *Property in Mediæval Theology.* Community of goods is said to be according to natural law in the canon law, but certain titles of acquiring private property are also said to be natural, so that the passage does not help the discussion very much (*Corp. Jur. Can.*, Dec. I. Dist. i. c. 7.

Secondly, because human affairs are conducted
in more orderly fashion if each man is charged
with taking care of some particular thing himself,
whereas there would be confusion if everybody
had to look after any one thing indeterminately.
Thirdly, because a more peaceful state is ensured
to man if each one is contented with his own.
Hence it is to be observed that quarrels more
frequently occur when there is no division of the
things possessed.'[1]   It is quite clear from this
passage that Aquinas regarded property as something essential to the existence of society in the
natural condition of human nature—that is to
say, the condition that it had acquired at the fall.
It is precisely the greed and avarice of fallen man
that renders property an indispensable institution.

There was another sense in which property was
said to be according to human law, in distinction
to the natural law, namely, in the sense that,
whereas the general principle that men should
own things might be said to be natural, the
particular proprietary rights of each individual
were determined by positive law.   In other words,
the *fundamentum* of property rights was natural,
whereas the *titulus* of particular property rights
was according to positive law.   This distinction
is stated clearly by Aquinas : [2]   ' The natural
right or just is that which by its very nature is
adjusted to or commensurate with another person.
Now this may happen in two ways ; first, according as it is considered absolutely ; thus the male
by its very nature is commensurate with the

[1] II. ii. 66, 2.   [2] II. ii. 57, 3.

female to beget offspring by her, and a parent is commensurate with the offspring to nourish it. Secondly, a thing is naturally commensurate with another person, not according as it is considered absolutely, but according to something resultant from it—for instance, the possession of property. For if a particular piece of land be considered absolutely, it contains no reason why it should belong to one man more than to another, but if it be considered in respect of its adaptability to cultivation, and the unmolested use of the land, it has a certain commensuration to be the property of one and not of another man, as the Philosopher shows.' Cajetan's commentary on this article clearly emphasises the distinction between *fundamentum* and *titulus* : ' In the ownership of goods two things are to be discussed. The first is why one thing should belong to one man and another thing to another. The second is why this particular field should belong to this man, that field to that man. With regard to the former inquiry, it may be said that the ownership of things is according to the law of nations, but with regard to the second, it may be said to result from the positive law, because in former times one thing was appropriated by one man and another thing by another.' It must not be supposed, however, from what we have just said, that there are no natural titles to property. Labour, for instance, is a title flowing from the natural law, as also is occupancy, and in certain circumstances, prescription. All that is meant by the distinction between *fundamentum* and *titulus* is that, whereas it can be clearly demonstrated by natural law that the goods of the earth, which are given by God for the benefit of the whole of mankind, cannot be made use of to their full advantage unless they are made the subject of private ownership, particular goods cannot be demonstrated to be the lawful property of this or that person unless some human act has intervened. This human act need not necessarily be an act of agreement ; it may equally be an act of some other kind—for instance, a decree of the law-giver, or the exercise of labour upon one's own goods. In the latter case, the additional value of the goods becomes the lawful property of the person who has exerted the labour. Aquinas therefore pronounced unmistakably in favour of the legitimacy of private property, and in doing so was in full agreement with the Fathers of the Church. He was followed without hesitation by all the later theologians, and it is abundantly evident from their writings that the right of private property was the keystone of their whole economic system.[1]

Communism therefore was no part of the scholastic teaching, but it must not be concluded from this that the mediævals approved of the unregulated individualism which modern opinion allows to the owners of property. The very strength of

---

[1] A community of goods, more or less complete, and a denial of the rights of private property was part of the teaching of many sects which were condemned as heretical—for instance, the Albigenses, the Vaudois, the Bégards, the Apostoli, and the Fratricelli. (See Brants, *op. cit.*, Appendix II.

the right to own property entailed as a consequence
the duty of making good use of it; and a clear
distinction was drawn between the power 'of
procuring and dispensing' property and the power
of using it. We have dealt with the former power
in the present section, and we shall pass to the
consideration of the latter in the next. In a
later chapter we shall proceed to discuss the
duties which attached to the owners of property
in regard to its exchange.

SECTION 2.—DUTIES REGARDING THE ACQUISITION AND USE OF PROPERTY

We referred at the end of the last section to the
very important distinction which Aquinas draws
between the power of procuring and dispensing [1]
exterior things and the power of using them.
'The second thing that is competent to man with
regard to external things is their use. In this
respect man ought to possess external things, not
as his own, but as common, so that, to wit, he is
ready to communicate them to others in their
need.' [2] These words wherein St. Thomas lays
down the doctrine of community of user of pro-

[1] Goyau insists on the importance of the words 'procure' and 'dispense.' 'Dont le premier éveille l'idée d'une constante sollicitude, et dont le second évoque l'image d'une générosité sympathetique' (*Autour du Catholicisme Sociale*, vol. ii. p. 93).

[2] II. ii. 66, 2. In another part of the *Summa* the same distinction is clearly laid down. 'Bona temporalia quæ homini divinitus conferuntur, ejus quidem sunt quantum ad proprietatem; sed quantum ad usum non solum desent esse ejus, sed aliorum qui en eis sustentari possunt en eo quod ei superfluit,' II. ii. 32, 5, ad 2.

perty were considered as authoritative by all
later writers on the subject, and were universally quoted with approval by them,[1] and may
therefore be taken as expressing the generally
held view of the Middle Ages. They require
careful explanation in order that their meaning
be accurately understood.[2] Cajetan's gloss on
this section of the *Summa* enables us to understand its significance in a broad sense, but fuller
information must be derived from a study of other
parts of the *Summa* itself. ' Note,' says Cajetan,
' that the words that community of goods in
respect of use arises from the law of nature may
be understood in two ways, one positively, the
other negatively. And if they are understood in
their positive sense they mean that the law of
nature dictates that all things are common to all
men ; if in their negative sense, that the law of
nature did not establish private ownership of
possessions. And in either sense the proposition
is true if correctly understood. In the first place,
if they are taken in their positive sense, a man
who is in a position of extreme necessity may take
whatever he can find to succour himself or another
in the same condition, nor is he bound in such a
case to restitution, because by natural law he has

[1] Janssen, *op. cit.*, vol. ii. p. 91.

[2] The Abbé Calippe summarises St. Thomas's doctrine as follows :
' Le droit de propriété est un droit réel; mais ce n'est pas un droit
illimité, les propriétaires ont des devoirs ; ils ont des devoirs parce que
Dieu qui a créé la terre ne l'a pas créée pour eux seuls, mais pour
tous ' (*Semaine Sociale de France*, 1909, p. 123). According to
Antoninus of Florence, goods could be evilly acquired, evilly distributed,
or evilly consumed (*Irish Theological Quarterly*, vol. vii. p. 146).

but made use of his own. And in the negative
sense they are equally true, because the law of
nature did not institute one thing the property
of one person, and another thing of another
person.' The principle of community of user
flows logically from the very nature of property
itself as defined by Aquinas, who taught that
the supreme justification of private property
was that it was the most advantageous method
of securing for the community the benefits of
material riches. While the owner of property
has therefore an absolute right to the goods he
possesses, he must at the same time remember
that this right is established primarily on his power
to benefit his neighbour by his proper use of it.
The best evidence of the correctness of this statement is the fact that the scholastics admitted
that, if the owner of property was withholding it
from the community, or from any member of the
community who had a real need of it, he could be
forced to apply it to its proper end. If the community could pay for it, it was bound to do so ;
but if the necessitous person could not pay for
it, he was none the less entitled to take it. The
former of these cases was illustrated by the
principle of the *dominium eminens* of the State ;
and the latter by the principle that the giving of
alms to a person in real need was a duty not of
charity, but of justice.[1] We shall see in a moment

---

[1] On the application of this principle by the popes in the thirteenth
and fifteenth centuries in the case of their own estates, see Ardant,
Papes et Paysans, a work which must be read with a certain degree of
caution (Nitti, *Catholic Socialism*, p. 290).

that the most usual application of the principle
enunciated by Aquinas was in the case of one
person's extreme necessity which required almsgiving from another's superfluity, but, even short of
such cases, there were rules of conduct in respect of
the user of property on all occasions which were
of extreme importance in the economic life of the
time.

These principles for the guidance of the owner of
property are not collected under any single head-
ing in the *Summa*, but must be gathered from the
various sections dealing with man's duty to his
fellow-men and to himself. One leading virtue
which was inculcated with great emphasis by
Aquinas was that of temperance. ' All pleasur-
able things which come within the use of man,'
we read in the section dealing with this subject,
' are ordered to some necessity of this life as an
end. And therefore temperance accepts the
necessity of this life as a rule or measure of the
things one uses, so that, to wit, they should be
used according as the necessity of this life requires.' [1] St. Thomas explains, moreover, that
' necessary ' must be taken in the broad sense of
suitable to one's condition of life, and not merely
necessary to maintain existence.[2] The principles
of temperance did not apply in any special way to
the user of property more than to the enjoyment

[1] II. ii. 141, 5.
[2] *Ibid.*, ad. 2. As Buridan puts it (*Eth.*, iv. 4), ' If any man has more
than is necessary for his own requirements, and does not give away
anything to the poor, and to his relations and neighbours, he is acting
against right reason.'

of any other good;[1] but they are relevant as laying down the broad test of right and wrong in the user of one's goods.

More particularly relevant to the subject before us is the teaching of Aquinas on liberality, which is a virtue directly connected with the user of property. Aquinas defines liberality as ' a virtue by which men use well all those exterior things which are given to us for sustenance.'[2] The limitations within which liberality should be practised are stated in the same article : ' As St. Basil and St. Ambrose say, God has given to many a superabundance of riches, in order that they might gain merit by their dispensing them well. Few things, however, suffice for one man ; and therefore the liberal man will advantageously expend more on others than on himself. In the spiritual sphere a man must always care for himself before his neighbours; and also in temporal things liberality does not demand that a man should think of others to the exclusion of himself and those dependent on him.'[3]

' It is not necessary for liberality that one should give away so much of one's riches that not enough remains to sustain himself and to enable him to perform works of virtue. This complete giving away without reserve belongs to the state of the perfection of spiritual life, of which we shall treat lower down ; but it must be known that to give

---

[1] ' Rationalis creaturæ vera perfectio est unamquamque rem tanti habere quanti habenda est, sicut pluris est anima quam esca ; fides et æquitas quam pecunia ' (Gerson, *De. Cont.*).

[2] II. ii. 117, 1.   [3] *Ibid.*, ad. 1.

one's goods liberally is an act of virtue which itself produces happiness.'[1] The author proceeds to discuss whether making use of money might be an act of liberality, and replies that 'as money is by its very nature to be classed among useful goods, because all exterior things are destined for the use of man, therefore the proper act of liberality is the good use of money and other riches.'[2] Moreover, ' it belongs to a virtuous man not simply to use well the goods which form the matter of his actions, but also to prepare the means and the occasions to use them well ; thus the brave soldier sharpens his blade and keeps it in the scabbard, as well as exercising it on the enemy ; in like manner, the liberal man should prepare and reserve his riches for a suitable use.'[3] It appears from this that to save part of one's annual income to provide against emergencies in the future, either by means of insurance or by investing in productive enterprises, is an act of liberality.

The question is then discussed whether liber-

[1] II. ii. 117, ad. 2.   [2] *Ibid.*, ad. 3.
[3] *Ibid.*, ad. 2.   ' Potest concludi quod accipere et custodire modificata sunt acta liberalitatis. . . . Major per hoc probatur quod dantem multotiens et consumentem, nihil autem accipientem et custodientem cito derelinqueret substantia temporalis ; et ita perirent omnis ejus actus quia non habent amplius quid dare et consumere. . . . Hic autem acceptio et custodia sic modificari debet. Primo quidem oportet ut non sit injusta ; secundo quod non sit de cupiditate vel avaritia suspecta propter excessum ; tertio quod non permittat labi substantiam propter defectum . . . Dare quando oportet et custodire quando oportet dare contrariantur ; sed dare quando oportet et custodire quando oportet non contrariantur ' (Buridan, *Eth.*, iv. 2).

ality is a part of justice. Aquinas concludes ' that liberality is not a species of justice, because justice renders to another what is his, but liberality gives him what is the giver's own. Still, it has a certain agreement with justice in two points ; first that it is to another, as justice also is ; secondly, that it is about exterior things like justice, though in another way. And therefore liberality is laid down by some to be a part of justice as a virtue annexed to justice as an accessory to a principal.' [1] Again, ' although liberality supposes not any legal debt as justice does, still it supposes a certain moral debt considering what is becoming in the person himself who practises the virtue, not as though he had any obligation to the other party ; and therefore there is about it very little of the character of a debt.' [2]

It is important to draw attention to the fact that *liberalitas* consists in making a good use of property, and not merely in distributing it to others, as a confusion with the English word 'liberality' might lead us to believe. It is, as we said above, therefore certain that a wise and prudent saving of money for investment would be considered a course of conduct within the meaning of the word *liberalitas*, especially if the enterprise in which the money were invested were one which would benefit the community as a whole. 'Modern industrial conditions demand that a man of wealth should distribute a part of his goods indirectly — that is, by investing

[1] II. ii. 117, art. 5. [2] *Ibid.*, ad. 1.

them in productive and labour-employing enterprises.' [1]

The nature of the virtue of *liberalitas* may be more clearly understood by an explanation of the vices which stand opposed to it. The first of these treated by Aquinas is avarice, which he defines as 'superfluus amor habendi divitias.' Avarice might be committed in two ways—by harbouring an undue desire of acquiring wealth, or by an undue reluctance to part with it—'primo autem superabundant in retinendo . . . secundo ad avaritiam pertinet superabundare in accipiendo.' [2] These definitions are amplified in another part of the same section. 'For in every action that is directed to the attainment of some end goodness consists in the observance of a certain measure. The means to the end must be commensurate with the end, as medicine with health. But exterior goods have the character of things needful to an end. Hence human goodness in the matter of these goods must consist in the observance of a certain measure, as is done by a man seeking to have exterior riches in so far as they are necessary to his life according to his rank and condition. And therefore sin consists in exceeding this measure and trying to acquire or retain riches beyond the due limit ; and this is the proper nature of avarice, which is defined to be an immoderate love of having.' [3] 'Avarice may involve immoderation regarding exterior

[1] Ryan, *The Alleged Socialism of the Church Fathers*, p. 20, and see Goyau, *Le Pape et la Question Sociale*, p. 79.
[2] II. ii. 118, 4.   [3] *Ibid.*, ad. 1.

things in two ways; in one way immediately
as to the receiving or keeping of them when one
acquires or keeps beyond the due amount; and
in this respect it is directly a sin against one's
neighbour, because in exterior things one man
cannot have superabundance without another
being in want, since temporal goods cannot be
simultaneously possessed by many. The other
way in which avarice may involve immoderation
is in interior affection. . . .' These words must
not be taken to condemn the acquisition of large
fortunes by capitalists, which is very often necessary in order that the natural resources of a
country may be properly exploited. One man's
possession of great wealth is at the present day
frequently the means of opening up new sources
of wealth and revenue to the entire community.
In other words, superabundance is a relative term.
This, like many other passages of St. Thomas,
must be given a *contemporanea expositio*. ' There
were no capitalists in the thirteenth century, but
only hoarders.' [1]

It must also be remembered that what would
be considered avarice in a man in one station of
life would not be considered such in a man in
another. So long as one did not attempt to
acquire an amount of wealth disproportionate to
the needs of one's station of life, one could not
be considered avaricious. Thus a common soldier
would be avaricious if he strove to obtain a
uniform of the quality worn by an officer, and a

---

[1] Rickaby, *Aquinas Ethicus*, vol. ii. p. 234.

simple cleric if he attempted to clothe himself in a style only befitting a bishop.[1]

The avaricious man offended against liberality by caring too much about riches; the prodigal, on the other hand, cared too little about them, and did not attach to them their proper value. ' In affection while the prodigal falls short, not taking due care of them, in exterior behaviour it belongs to the prodigal to exceed in giving, but to fail in keeping or acquiring, while it belongs to the miser to come short in giving, but to superabound in getting and in keeping. Therefore it is clear that prodigality is the opposite of covetousness.' [2] A man, however, might commit both sins at the same time, by being unduly anxious to acquire wealth which he distributed prodigally.[3] Prodigality could always be distinguished from extreme liberality by a consideration of the circumstances of the particular case ; a truly liberal man might give away more than a prodigal in case of necessity.[4] Prodigality, though a sin, was a sin of a less grievous kind than avarice.[5]

---

[1] Aquinas, *In Orat. Dom. Expos.*, iv.   Ashley gives many quotations from early English literature to show how fully the idea of *status* was accepted (*Economic History*, vol. i. pt. ii. p. 389).   On the warfare waged by the Church on luxury in the Middle Ages, see Baudrillard, *Histoire du Luxe privé et publique*, vol. iii. pp. 630 *et seq.*

[2] II. ii. 119, 1.

[3] *Ibid.*, ad. 1.   [4] *Ibid.*, ad. 3.

[5] *Ibid.*, art. 3.   ' Per prodigalitatem intelligimus habitum quo quis præter vel contra dictamen rectae rationis circa pecunias excedit in datione vel consumptione vel custodia ; et per illiberalitatem intelligimus habitum quo quis contra dictamen rectae rationis deficit circa pecunias in datione vel consumptione, vel superabundat in acceptione vel custodia ipsarum ' (Buridan, *Eth.*, iv. 3).

In addition to the duties which were imposed on the owners of property in all circumstances there was, a further duty which only arose on special occasions, namely, *magnificentia*, or munificence. This virtue is discussed by Aquinas,[1] but we shall quote the passages of Buridan which explain it, not because they depart in any way from the teaching of Aquinas, but because they are clearer and more scientific. ' By munificence, we understand a habit inclining one to the performance of great works, or to the incurring of great expenses, when, where, and in the manner in which they are called for (*fuerit opportunum*), for example, building a church, assembling great armies for a threatened war, and giving splendid marriage feasts.' He explains that ' munificence stands in the same relation to liberality as bravery acquired by its exercise in danger of death in battle does to bravery simply and commonly understood.' Two vices stand opposed to munificentia : (1) *parvificentia*, ' a habit inclining one not to undertake great works, when circumstances call for them, or to undertaking less, or at less expense, than the needs of the situation demand,' and (2) βανουσία, ' a habit inclining one to undertaking great works, which are not called for by circumstances, or undertaking them on a greater scale or at a greater expense than is necessary.' [2]

Both in the case of avarice and prodigality the offending state of mind consisted in attaching a wrong value to wealth, and the inculcation of

[1] II. ii. 134.　　　　　　　　[2] *Eth.*, iv. 7.

the virtue of liberality must have been attended
with good results not alone to the souls of individuals, but to the economic condition of the
community. The avaricious man not only im-
perilled his own soul by attaching too much
importance to temporal gain, but he also injured
the community by monopolising too large a share
of its wealth ; the prodigal man, in addition to
incurring the occasion of various sins of intemper-
ance, also impoverished the community by wast-
ing in reckless consumption wealth which might
have been devoted to productive or charitable
purposes. He who neglected the duty of munificence, either by refusing to make a great expenditure when it was called for (*parvificentia*) or by
making one when it was unnecessary (βανουσία)
was also deemed to have done wrong, because in
the one case he valued his money too highly, and
in the other not highly enough. In other words,
he attached a wrong value to wealth. Nothing
could be further from the truth than the suggestion that the schoolmen despised or belittled
temporal riches. Quite on the contrary, they
esteemed it a sin to conduct oneself in a manner
which showed a defective appreciation of their
value.[1] Riches may have been the occasion of
sin ; but so was poverty. ' The occasions of sin
are to be avoided,' says Aquinas, ' but poverty
is an occasion of evil, because theft, perjury, and
flattery are frequently brought about by it.

---

[1] ' Non videtur secundum humanam rationem esse boni et perfecti
divitias abjicere totaliter, sed eis uti bene et reficiendo superfluas
pauperibus subvenire et amicis ' (Buridan, *Eth.*, iv. 3).

Therefore poverty should not be voluntarily
undertaken, but rather avoided.'[1] Buridan says:
' There is no doubt that it is much more difficult
to be virtuous in a state of poverty than in one
of moderate affluence ; '[2] and Antoninus of
Florence expresses the opinion that poverty is in
itself an evil thing, although out of it good may
come.[3] Even the ambition to rise in the world
was laudable, because every one may rightfully
desire to place himself and his dependants in a
participation of the fullest human felicity of which
man is capable, and to rid himself of the necessity
of corporal labour.[4] Avarice and prodigality
alike offended against liberality, because they
tended to deprive the community of the maximum
benefit which it should derive from the wealth
with which it was endowed. Dr. Cunningham
may be quoted in support of this view. ' One of
the gravest defects of the Roman Empire lay in
the fact that its system left little scope for individual aims, and tended to check the energy of
capitalists and labourers alike. But Christian
teaching opened up an unending prospect before
the individual personally, and encouraged him to
activity and diligence by an eternal hope. Nor
did such concentration of thought on a life beyond the grave necessarily divert attention from
secular duties ; Christianity did not disparage
them, but set them in a new light, and brought
out new motives for taking them seriously. . . .
The acceptance of this higher view of the dignity

[1] *Summa cont. Gent.*, iii. 131. [2] *Eth.*, iv. 3.
[3] *Summa*, iv. 12, 3. [4] Cajetan, *Comm.* on II. ii. 118, 1.

of human life as immortal was followed by a fuller recognition of personal responsibility. Ancient philosophy had seen that man is the master of material things ; but Christianity introduced a new sense of duty in regard ı⊃ the manner of using them. . . . Christian teachers were forced to protest against any employment of wealth that disregarded the glory of God and the good of man.'[1] It was the opinion of Knies that the peculiarly Christian virtues were of profound economic value. ' Temperance, thrift, and industry—that is to say, the sun and rain of economic activity—were recommended by the Church and inculcated as Christian virtues ; idleness as the mother of theft, gambling as the occasion of fraud, were forbidden ; and gain for its own sake was classed as a kind of robbery.'[2]

The great rule, then, with regard to the user of property was liberality. Closely allied with the duty of liberality was the duty of almsgiving—' an act of charity through the medium of money.'[3] Almsgiving is not itself a part of liberality except in so far as liberality removes an obstacle to such acts, which may arise from excessive love of riches, the result of which is that one clings to them more than one ought.[4] Aquinas divides

---

[1] *Western Civilisation*, vol. ii. pp. 8-9.

[2] *Politische Oekonomie vom Standpuncte der geschichtlichen Methode*, p. 116, and see Rambaud, *Histoire*, p. 759; Champagny, *La Bible et l'Economie politique* ; Thomas Aquinas, *Summa*, ii. ii. 50, 3 ; Sertillanges, *Socialisme et Christianisme*, p. 53. It was nevertheless recognised and insisted on that wealth was not an end in itself, but merely a means to an end (Aquinas, *Summa*, i. ii. 2, 1).

[3] ii. ii. 32, 1.   [4] *Ibid.*, ad. 4.

alms-deeds into two kinds, spiritual and corporal,
the latter alone of which concern us here.
'Corporal need arises either during this life or
afterwards. If it occurs during this life, it is
either a common need in respect of things needed
by all, or is a special need occurring through some
accident supervening. In the first case the need
is either internal or external. Internal need is
twofold : one which is relieved by solid food, viz.
hunger, in respect of which we have to *feed the
hungry* ; while the other is relieved by liquid
food, viz. thirst, in respect of which we have to
give drink to the thirsty. The common need with
regard to external help is twofold : one in respect
of clothing, and as to this we have to *clothe the
naked* ; while the other is in respect of a dwelling-
place, and as to this we have to *harbour the harbour-
less.* Again, if the need be special, it is either the
result of an internal cause like sickness, and then
we have to *visit the sick,* or it results from an
external cause, and then we have to *ransom the
captive.* After this life we *give burial to the dead.*' [1]
Aquinas then proceeds to explain in what circumstances the duty of almsgiving arises. ' Almsgiving is a matter of precept. Since, however,
precepts are about acts of virtue, it follows that
all almsgiving must be a matter of precept in so
far as it is necessary to virtue, namely, in so far
as it is demanded by right reason. Now right
reason demands that we should take into consideration something on the part of the giver, and something on the part of the recipient. On the part

[1] II. ii. 32, art. 2.

of the giver it must be noted that he must give
of his surplus according to Luke xi. 4, "That
which remaineth give alms." This surplus is to be
taken in reference not only to the giver, but also
in reference to those of whom he has charge (in
which case we have the expression *necessary to the
person*, taking the word *person* as expressive of
dignity). . . . On the part of the recipient it is
necessary that he should be in need, else there
would be no reason for giving him alms; yet
since it is not possible for one individual to relieve
the needs of all, we are not bound to relieve all
who are in need, but only those who could not be
succoured if we did not succour them. For in
such cases the words of Ambrose apply, "Feed him
that is dying of hunger; if thou hast not fed him
thou hast slain him." Accordingly we are bound
to give alms of our surplus, as also to give alms to
one whose need is extreme; otherwise almsgiving,
like any other greater good, is a matter of counsel.' [1]
In replying to the objection that it is lawful for
every one to keep what is his own, St. Thomas
restates with emphasis the principle of community
of user : ' The temporal goods which are given
us by God are ours as to the ownership, but as
to the use of them they belong not to us alone, but
also to such others as we are able to succour out
of what we have over and above our needs.' [2]
Albertus Magnus states this in very strong
words : 'For a man to give out of his superflu-
ities is a mere act of justice, because he is rather
then steward of them for the poor than the

[1] II. ii. 32, art. 5.   [2] *Ibid.*, ad. 2.

owner;'[1] and at an earlier date St. Peter Damian
had affirmed that 'he who gives to the poor returns what he does not himself own, and does not
dispose of his own goods.' He insists in the same
passage that almsgiving is not an act of mercy, but
of strict justice.[2] In the reply to another objection the duty of almsgiving is stated by Aquinas
with additional vigour. 'There is a time when we
sin mortally if we omit to give alms—on the part
of the recipient when we see that his need is evident and urgent, and that he is not likely to be
succoured otherwise—on the part of the giver
when he has superfluous goods, which he does not
need for the time being, so far as he can judge with
probability.'[3]

The next question which St. Thomas discusses
is whether one ought to give alms out of what one
needs. He distinguishes between two kinds of
'necessaries.' The first is that without which
existence is impossible, out of which kind of
necessary things one is not bound to give alms
save in exceptional cases, when, by doing so, one
would be helping a great personage or supporting
the Church or the State, since 'the common good
is to be preferred to one's own.' The second kind
of necessaries are those things without which a
man cannot live in keeping with his social station.
St. Thomas recommends the giving of alms out
of this part of one's estate, but points out that it
is only a matter of counsel, and not of precept,
and one must not give alms to such an extent as

[1] Jarrett, *Mediæval Socialism*, p. 87.
[2] *De Eleemosynis*, cap. 1.   [3] II. ii. 32, 5, ad. 3.

to impoverish oneself permanently.   To this last
provision, however, there are three exceptions :
one, when a man is entering religion and giving
away all his goods ; two, when he can easily
replace what he gives away ; and, three, when he
is in presence of great indigence on the part of an
individual, or great need on the part of the common weal. In these three cases it is praiseworthy
for a man to forgo the requisites of his station
in order to provide for a greater need.[1]

The mediæval teaching on almsgiving is very
well summarised by Fr. Jarrett,[2] as follows :
' (1) A man is obliged to help another in his extreme
need even at the risk of grave inconvenience to
himself ; (2) a man is obliged to help another who,
though not in extreme need, is yet in considerable
distress, but not at the risk of grave inconvenience
to himself ; (3) a man is not obliged to help another when necessity is slight, even though the
risk to himself should be quite trifling.'

The importance of the duty of almsgiving
further appears from the section where Aquinas
lays down that the person to whom alms should
have been given may, if the owner of the goods
neglects his duty, repair the omission himself.
' All things are common property in a case of
extreme necessity. Hence one who is in dire
straits may take another's goods in order to
succour himself if he can find no one who is willing
to give him something.'[3] The duty of using
one's goods for the benefit of one's neighbours

[1] II. ii. 32, 6.   [2] *Mediæval Socialism*, p. 90.
[3] *Ibid.*, art. 7 ad. 3.

was a fit matter for enforcement by the State,
provided that the burdens imposed by legislation
were equitable. ' Laws are said to be just, both
from the end, when, to wit, they are ordained to
the common good—and from their author, that
is to say, when the law that is made does not
exceed the power of the law-giver—and from their
form, when, to wit, burdens are laid on the subjects according to an equality of proportion and
with a view to the common good. For, since every
man is part of the community, each man in all
that he is and has belongs to the community :
just as a part in all that it is belongs to the whole ;
wherefore nature inflicts a loss on the part in order
to save the whole ; so that on this account such
laws, which impose proportionate burdens, are
just and binding in conscience.' [1]

There can be no doubt that the practice of
the scholastic teaching of community of user, in
its proper sense, made for social stability. The
following passage from Trithemius, written at the
end of the fifteenth century, is interesting as
showing how consistently the doctrine of St.
Thomas was adhered to two hundred years after
his death, and also that the failure of the rich
to put into practice the moderate communism
of St. Thomas was the cause of the rise of the
heretical communists, who attacked the very
foundations of property itself : ' Let the rich
remember that their possessions have not been
entrusted to them in order that they may have
the sole enjoyment of them, but that they may

[1] I. ii. 96, 4.

use and manage them as property belonging to mankind at large. Let them remember that when they give to the needy they only give them what belongs to them. If the duty of right use and management of property, whether worldly or spiritual, is neglected, if the rich think that they are the sole lords and masters of that which they possess, and do not treat the needy as their brethren, there must of necessity arise an inner shattering of the commonwealth. False teachers and deceivers of the people will then gain influence, as has happened in Bohemia, by preaching to the people that earthly property should be equally distributed among all, and that the rich must be forcibly condemned to the division of their wealth. Then follow lamentable conditions and civil wars ; no property is spared ; no right of ownership is any longer recognised ; and the wealthy may then with justice complain of the loss of possessions which have been unrighteously taken from them ; but they should also seriously ask themselves the question whether in the days of peace and order they recognised in the administration of these goods the right of their superior lord and owner, namely, the God of all the earth.' [1]

It must not, however, be imagined for a moment that the community of user advocated by the scholastics had anything in common with the communism recommended by modern Socialists. As we have seen above, the scholastic communism did not at all apply to the procuring and dispensing of material things, but only to the mode of

[1] Quoted in Janssen, *op. cit.*, vol. ii. p. 91.

using them. It is not even correct to say that
the property of an individual was *limited* by the
duty of using it for the common good. As
Rambaud puts it: 'Les devoirs de charité, d'équité
naturelle, et de simple convenance sociale peuvent
affecter, ou mieux encore, commander un certain
usage de la richesse, mais ce n'est pas le même
chose que limiter la propriété.'¹ The community
of user of the scholastics was distinguished from
that of modern Socialists not less strongly by the
motives which inspired it than by the effect it
produced. The former was dictated by high
spiritual aims, and the contempt of material goods;
the latter is the fruit of over-attachment to material goods, and the envy of their possessors.²

The large estates which the Church itself owned
have frequently been pointed to as evidence of
hypocrisy in its attitude towards the common
user of property. This is not the place to inquire
into the condition of ecclesiastical estates in the
Middle Ages, but it is sufficient to say that they
were usually the centres of charity, and that in
the opinion of so impartial a writer as Roscher,
they rather tended to make the rules of using

¹ *Op. cit.*, p. 43. The same writer shows that there is no authority
in Christian teaching for the proposition, advanced by many Christian
Socialists, that property is a 'social function' (*ibid.*, p. 774). The
right of property even carried with it the *jus abutendi*, which, however,
did not mean the right to *abuse*, but the right to destroy by consumption (see Antoine, *Cours d'Economie sociale*, p. 526).

² Roscher, *op. cit.*, p. 5: 'Vom neuern Socialismus freilich unter-
scheidet sich diese Auffassung nicht blosz durch ihre religiöse Grundlage,
sondern auch durch ihre, jedem Mammonsdienst entgegengesetze,
Verachtung der materiellen Güter.'

goods for the common use practicable than the contrary.[1]

SECTION 3.—PROPERTY IN HUMAN BEINGS

Before we pass from the subject of property, we must deal with a particular kind of property right, namely, that of one human being over another. At the present day the idea of one man being owned by another is repugnant to all enlightened public opinion, but this general repugnance is of very recent growth, and did not exist in mediæval Europe. In dealing with the scholastic attitude towards slavery, we shall indicate, as we did with regard to its attitude towards property in general, the fundamental harmony between the teaching of the primitive and the mediæval Church on the subject. No apology is needed for this apparent digression, as a comparison of the teaching of the Church at the two periods of its development helps us to understand precisely what the later doctrine was; and, moreover, the close analogy which, as we shall see, existed between the Church's view of property and slavery, throws much light on the true nature of both institutions.

Although in practice Christianity had done a very great deal to mitigate the hardships of the slavery of ancient times, and had in a large degree abolished slavery by its encouragement of emancipation,[2] it did not, in theory, object to the institu-

---

[1] Roscher, *op. cit.*, p. 6.

[2] See Roscher, *Political Economy*, s. 73.

tion itself. There is no necessity to labour a
point so universally admitted by all students of
the Gospels as that Christ and His Apostles did
not set out to abolish the slavery which they
found everywhere around them, but rather aimed,
by preaching charity to the master and patience
to the slave, at the same time to lighten the
burden of servitude, and to render its acceptance
a merit rather than a disgrace. ' What, in fact,'
says Janet, ' is the teaching of St. Peter, St. Paul,
and the Apostles in general ? It is, in the first
place, that in Christ there are no slaves, and that
all men are free and equal ; and, in the second
place, that the slave must obey his master, and
the master must be gentle to his slave.[1] Thus,
although there are no slaves in Christ, St. Paul
and the Apostles do not deny that there may be
on earth. I am far from reproaching the Apostles
for not having proclaimed the immediate necessity of the emancipation of slaves. But I say
that the question was discussed in precisely the
same terms by the ancient philosophers of the
same period. Seneca, it is true, proclaimed not
the civil, but the moral equality of men ; but
St. Paul does not speak of anything more than
their equality in Christ. Seneca instructs the
master to treat the slave as he would like to be
treated himself.[2] Is not this what St. Peter and
St. Paul say when they recommended the master
to be gentle and good ? The superiority of
Christianity over Stoicism in this question arises
altogether from the very superiority of the

[1] *Eph.*, vi. 5, 6, 9.   [2] *Ep. ad Luc.*, 73.

Christian spirit. . . .' [1]   The article on 'Slavery'
in the *Catholic Encyclopædia* expresses the same
opinion : ' Christian teachers, following the example of St. Paul, implicitly accept slavery as
not in itself incompatible with the Christian law.
The Apostle counsels slaves to obey their masters,
and to bear with their condition patiently. This
estimate of slavery continued to prevail until it
became fixed in the systematised ethical teaching of the schools ; and so it remained without
any conspicuous modification until the end of
the eighteenth century.' The same interpretation
of early Christian teaching is accepted by the
Protestant scholar, Dr. Bartlett : ' The practical
attitude of Seneca and the early Christians to
slavery was much the same. They bade the individual rise to a sense of spiritual freedom in spite
of outward bondage, rather than denounce the
institution as an altogether illegitimate form of
property.' [2]

Several texts might be collected from the
writings of the Fathers which would seem to show
that according to patristic teaching the institution of slavery was unjustifiable. We do not
propose to cite or to explain these texts one by
one, in view of the quite clear and unambiguous
exposition of the subject given by St. Thomas

---

[1] Janet, *op. cit.*, p. 317.

[2] ' Biblical and Early Christian Idea of Property,' *Property, Its
Duties and Rights* (London, 1915), p. 110; Franck, *Réformateurs et
Publicistes de l'Europe : Moyen âge*—Renaissance, p. 87. On the whole
question by far the best authority is volume iii. of Wallon's *Histoire
de l'Esclavage dans l'Antiquité*.

Aquinas, whose teaching is the more immediate
subject of this essay ; we shall content ourselves
by reminding the reader of the precisely similar
texts relating to the institution of property which
we have examined above, and by stating that the
corresponding texts on the subject of slavery are
capable of an exactly similar interpretation. ' The
teaching of the Apostle,' says Janet, ' and of the
Fathers on slavery is the same as their teaching
on property.' [1] The author from whom we are
quoting, and on whose judgment too much
reliance cannot be placed, then proceeds to cite
many of the patristic texts on property, which we
quoted in the section dealing with that subject,
and asks : ' What conclusion should one draw
from these different passages ? It is that in
Christ there are no rich and no poor, no mine and
no thine ; that in Christian perfection all things
are common to all men, but that nevertheless
property is legitimate and derived from human
law. Is it not in the same sense that the Fathers
condemned slavery as contrary to divine law,
while respecting it as comfortable to human law ?
The Fathers abound in texts contrary to slavery,
but have we not seen a great number of texts
contrary to property ? ' [2] The closeness of the
analogy between the patristic treatment of slavery
and of property appears forcibly in the following
passage of Lactantius : ' God who created man
willed that all should be equal. He has imposed
on all the same condition of living ; He has produced all in wisdom ; He has promised immortality

[1] *Op. cit.*, p. 318.   [2] *Ibid.*, p. 321.

to all; no one is cut off from His heavenly benefits. In His sight no one is a slave, no one a master; for if we have all the same Father, by an equal right we are all His children; no one is poor in the sight of God but he who is without justice, no one rich but he who is full of virtue. . . . Some one will say, Are there not among you some poor and others rich; some servants and others masters ?. Is there not some difference between individuals? There is none, nor is there any other cause why we mutually bestow on each other the name of brethren except that we believe ourselves to be equal. For since we measure all human things not by the body but by the spirit, although the condition of bodies is different, yet we have no servants, but we both regard them, and speak of them as brothers in spirit, in religion as fellow-servants.' [1] Slavery was declared to be a blessing, because, like poverty, it afforded the opportunity of practising the virtues of humility and patience. [2]

The treatment of the institution of slavery underwent a striking and important development in the hands of St. Augustine, who justified it as one of the penalties incurred by man as a result of the sin of Adam and Eve. 'The first holy men,' writes the Saint, 'were rather shepherds than kings, God showing herein what both the order of the creation desired, and what the deserts of sin exacted. For justly was the burden of servitude laid upon the back of transgression. And therefore in all the Scriptures we never read

[1] *Div. Inst.*, v. 15-16.
[2] Chryst., *Genes.*, serm. v. i.; *Ep. ad Cor.*, hom. xix. 4.

the word *servus* until Noah laid it as a curse upon
his offending son. So that it was guilt, and not
nature, that gave origin to that name. . . . Sin is
the mother of servitude and the first cause of
man's subjection to man.' [1] St. Augustine also
justifies the enslavement of those conquered in
war—' It is God's decree to humble the conquered,
either reforming their sins herein or punishing
them.' [2]

Janet ably analyses and expounds the advance
which St. Augustine made in the treatment of
slavery : ' In this theory we must note the
following points : (1) Slavery is unjust according
to the law of nature. This is what is contrary
to the teaching of Aristotle, but conformable to
that of the Stoics. (2) Slavery is just as a consequence of sin. This is the new principle peculiar
to St. Augustine. He has found a principle of
slavery, which is neither natural inequality, nor
war, nor agreement, but sin. Slavery is no more
a transitory fact which we accept provisionally,
so as not to precipitate a social revolution : it is
an institution which has become natural as a result
of the corruption of our nature. (3) It must not
be said that slavery, resulting from sin, is destroyed by Christ who destroyed sin. . . . Slavery,
according to St. Augustine, must last as long as
society.' [3]

Nowhere does St. Thomas Aquinas appear as
clearly as the medium of contact and reconciliation
between the Fathers of the Church and the ancient

---

[1] *De Civ. Dei*, xix. 14-15. [2] *Ibid.*

[3] Janet, *op. cit.*, p. 302.

philosophers as in his treatment of the question of slavery. His utterances upon this subject are scattered through many portions of his work, but, taken together, they show that he was quite prepared to admit the legitimacy of the institution, not alone on the grounds put forward by St. Augustine, but also on those suggested by Aristotle and the Roman jurists.

He fully adopts the Augustinian argument in the *Summa*, where, in answer to the query, whether in the state of innocence all men were equal, he states that even in that state there would still have been inequalities of sex, knowledge, justice, etc. The only inequalities which would not have been present were those arising from sin ; but the only inequality arising from sin was slavery.[1] ' By the words " So long as we are without sin we are equal," Gregory means to exclude such inequality as exists between virtue and vice ; the result of which is that some are placed in subjection to others as a penalty.'[2] In the following article St. Thomas distinguishes between political and despotic subordination, and shows that the former might have existed in a state of innocence. ' Mastership has a twofold meaning ; first as opposed to servitude, in which case a master means one to whom another is subject as a slave. In another sense mastership is commonly referred to any kind of subject ; and in that sense even he who has the office of governing and directing free men can be called a master. In the first meaning of mastership man would not

[1] i. 96, 3.   [2] *Ibid.*, ad. 1.

have been ruled by man in the state of innocence ; but in the latter sense man would be ruled over by man in that state.' [1] In *De Regimine Principum* Aquinas also accepts what we may call the Augustinian view of slavery. 'But whether the dominion of man over man is according to the law of nature, or is permitted or provided by God may be certainly resolved. If we speak of dominion by means of servile subjection, this was introduced because of sin. But if we speak of dominion in so far as it relates to the function of advising and directing, it may in this sense be said to be natural.' [2]

St. Thomas was therefore willing to endorse the argument of St. Augustine that slavery was a result of sin; but he also admits the justice of Aristotle's reasoning on the subject. In the section of the *Summa* where the question is discussed, whether the law of nations is the same as the natural law, one of the objections to be met is that 'Slavery among men is natural, for some are naturally slaves according to the philosopher. Now "slavery belongs to the law of nations," as Isidore states. Therefore the right of nations is a natural right.' [3] In answer to this objection St. Thomas draws the distinction between what is natural absolutely, and what is natural *secundum quid*, the passage which we have quoted in treating of property rights. [4] He then goes on to

---

[1] i. 96, 4.

[2] *De Reg. Prin.*, iii. 9. This is one of the chapters the authorship of which is disputed.

[3] II. ii. 57, 3.   [4] *Supra*, p. 64.

apply this distinction to the case of slavery. 'Considered absolutely, the fact that this particular man should be a slave rather than another man, is based, not on natural reason, but on some resultant utility, in that it is useful to this man to be ruled by a wise man, and to the latter to be helped by the former, as the philosopher states. Wherefore slavery which belongs to the law of nations is natural in the second way, but not in the first.' [1] It will be noted from this passage that St. Thomas partly admits, though not entirely, the opinion of Aristotle. In the *De Regimine Principum* he goes much further in the direction of adopting the full Aristotelian theory : 'Nature decrees that there should be grades in men as in other things. We see this in the elements, a superior and an inferior ; we see in every mixture that some one element predominates. . . . For we see this also in the relation of the body and the mind, and in the powers of the mind compared with one another ; because some are ordained towards ordering and moving, such as the understanding and the will ; others to serving. So should it be among men ; and thus it is proved that some are slaves according to nature. Some lack reason through some defect of nature ; and such ought to be subjected to servile works because they cannot use their reason, and this is called the natural law.' [2] In the same chapter the right of conquerors to enslave their conquered is referred to without comment, and therefore implicitly approved by the author.

[1] II. ii. 57, ad. 2.　　　　[2] *De Reg. Prin.*, ii. 10.

'Thus,' according to Janet, 'St. Thomas admits slavery as far as one can admit it, and for all the reasons for which one can admit it. He admits with Aristotle that there is a natural slavery; with St. Augustine that slavery is the result of sin; with the jurisconsult that slavery is the result of war and convention.'[1] 'The author justifies slavery,' says Franck, 'in the name of St. Augustine, and in that of Aristotle; in the name of the latter by showing that there are two races of men, one born to command, and the other to obey; in the name of the former in affirming that slavery had its origin in original sin; that by sin man has forfeited his right to liberty. Further, we must admit slavery as an institution not only of nature and one of the consequences of the fall, we must admit a third principle of slavery which appears to St. Thomas as legitimate as the other two. War is necessary; therefore it is just; and if it is just we must accept its consequences. One of these consequences is the absolute right of the conqueror over the life, person, and goods of the conquered.'[2]

Aquinas returns to the question of slavery in another passage, which is interesting as showing that he continued to make use of the analogy between slavery and property which we have seen in the Fathers. 'A thing is said to belong to the natural law in two ways. First, because nature inclines thereto, e.g. that one should not do harm to another. Secondly, because nature did not bring in the contrary; thus we might say that

[1] *Op. cit.*, vol. i. p. 431.　　　[2] Franck, *op cit.*, p. 69.

for man to be naked is of the natural law because nature did not give him clothes, but art invented them. In this sense the possession of all things in common and universal freedom is said to be of the natural law, because, to wit, the distinction of possession and slavery were not brought in by nature, but devised by human reason for the benefit of human life. Accordingly, the law of nature was not changed in this respect, but by addition.'[1]

Ægidius Romanus closely follows the teaching of his master on the subject of slavery. 'What does Ægidius do ? He unites Aristotle and St. Augustine against human liberty. He declares with the latter that man has lost the right of belonging to himself, since he has fallen from the primitive order established by God Himself in nature. He admits with Aristotle the existence of two races of men, the one designed for liberty, the other for servitude. . . . This is not all—to this servitude which he calls natural, the author joins another, purely legal, but which does not seem to him less just, namely, that which is founded on the right of war, and which obliges the conquered to become the slaves of the conquerors—to give up their liberty in exchange for their lives. Our author admits it is just in itself, because in his opinion it is useful to the defence of one's country ; it excites warriors to courage by placing before their eyes the terrible consequences of cowardice.'[2] The teachings of St. Thomas and Ægidius were accepted by all the

[1] I. ii. 94, 5, ad. 3.　　　　　[2] Franck, *op cit.*, p. 90.

later scholastics.[1] Biel, whose opinion is always very valuable as being that of the last of a long line, says that there are three kinds of slaves— slaves of God, of sin, and of man. The first kind of slavery is wholly good, the second wholly bad, while the third, though not instituted by, is approved by the *jus gentium*. He proceeds to state the four ways in which a man may become enslaved : namely, *ex necessitate*, or by being born of a slave mother ; *ex bello*, by being captured in war ; *ex delicto*, or by sentence of the law in the case of certain crimes committed by freedmen ; and *ex propria voluntate*, or by the sale of a man of himself into slavery.[2]

It must not be forgotten that we are dealing purely with theory. In fact the Church did an inestimable amount of good to the servile classes, and, at the time that Aquinas wrote, thanks to the operation of Christianity in this respect, the old Roman slavery had completely disappeared. The nearest approach to ancient slavery in the Middle Ages was serfdom, which was simply a step in the transition from slavery to free labour.[3] Moreover, the rights of the master over the slave were strictly confined to the disposal of his services ; the ancient absolute right over his body had completely disappeared. ' In those things,' says St. Thomas, ' which appertain to the disposition of human acts and things, the subject is

---

[1] Franck, *op. cit.*, p. 91.

[2] Biel, *Inventarium seu Repertorium generale super quatuor libros Sententiarum*, IV. xv. 1 ; and see Carletus, *Summa Angelica*, q. ccxii.

[3] Wallon, *op. cit.*, vol. iii. p. 93 ; Brants, *op. cit.*, p. 87.

bound to obey his superior according to the reason
of the superiority ; thus a soldier must obey his
officer in those things which appertain to war ;
a slave his master in those things which appertain to the carrying out of his servile works.'[1]
'Slavery does not abolish the natural equality of
man,' says a writer who is quoted by the *Catholic
Encyclopædia* as correctly stating the Catholic
doctrine on the subject prior to the eighteenth
century, ' hence by slavery one man is understood
to become subject to the dominion of another to
the extent that the master has a perfect right to
the services which one man may justly perform
for another.'[2]   Biel, who lays down the justice of
slavery so unambiguously, is no less clear in his
statement of the limitations of the right.   ' The
body of the slave is not simply in the power of the
master as the body of an ox is ; nor can the
master kill or mutilate the slave, nor abuse him
contrary to the law of God.   The temporal gains
derived from the labour of the slave belong to
the master ; but the master is bound to provide
the slave with the necessaries of life.'[3]   Rambaud
very properly points out that the reason that the
scholastic writers did not fulminate in as strong
and as frequent language against the tyranny of
masters, was not that they felt less strongly on
the subject, but that the abuses of the ancient
slave system had almost entirely disappeared
under the influence of Christian teaching.[4]

On the other hand, it must not be imagined, as

[1] II. ii. 104, 5.

[2] Gerdil., *Comp. Inst. Civ. I.*, vii.

[3] Biel, *op. cit.*, IV. xv. 5.

[4] *Op. cit.*, p. 83.

has sometimes been suggested, that the slavery defended by Aquinas was not real slavery, but rather the ordinary modern relation between employer and employed. Such an interpretation is definitely disproved by a passage of the article on justice where Aquinas says that ' inducing a slave to leave his master is properly an injury against the person . . . and, since the slave is his master's chattel, it is referred to theft.' [1]

[1] II. ii. 61, 3. Brants, *op. cit.*, pp. 87 *et seq.*, is inclined to take a more liberal view of the scholastic doctrine on slavery, but we cannot agree with him in view of the contemporary texts.

CHAPTER III

DUTIES REGARDING THE EXCHANGE OF PROPERTY

SECTION 1.—THE SALE OF GOODS

§ 1. *The Just Price*

WE dealt in the last chapter with the duties which attached to property in respect of its acquisition and use, and we now pass to the duties which attached to it in respect of its exchange. As we indicated above, the right to exchange one's goods for the goods or the money of another person was, according to the scholastics, one of the necessary corollaries of the right of private property. In order that such exchange might be justifiable, it must be conducted on a basis of commutative justice, which, as we have seen, consisted in the observance of equality according to the arithmetical mean. We further drew attention to the fact that exchanges might be divided into sales of goods and sales of the use of money. In the former case the regulating principle of the equality of justice was given effect to by the observance of the *just price* ; in the latter by that of the *prohibition of usury*. We shall deal with

the former in the present and with the latter in
the following section.

The mediæval teaching on the just price,
about which there has been so much discussion
and disagreement among modern writers, was
simply the application to the particular contract
of sale of the principles which regulated contracts
in general. Exchange originally took the form
of barter ; but, as it was found impossible accurately to measure the values of the objects
exchanged without the intervention of some
common measure of value, money was invented
to serve as such a measure. We need not further
refer to barter in this section, as the principles
which applied to it were those that applied to
sale. Indeed all sales when analysed are really
barter through the medium of money. That
Aquinas simply regarded his article on just price [1]
as an explanation of the application of his general
teaching on justice to the particular case of the
contract of sale is quite clear from the article
itself. 'Apart from fraud, we may speak of
buying and selling in two ways. First, as considered in themselves ; and from this point of view
buying and selling seem to be established for the
common advantage of both parties, one of whom
requires that which belongs to the other, and
vice versa. Now whatever is established for the
common advantage should not be more of a
burden to one part than to the other, and consequently all contracts between them should observe
equality of thing and thing. Again, the quality

[1] ii. ii. 77, 1.

of a thing that comes into human use is measured by the price given for it, for which purpose money was invented. Therefore, if either the price exceed the quantity of the thing's worth, or conversely the worth of the thing exceed the price, there is no longer the equality of justice ; and consequently to sell a thing for more than its worth, or to buy it for less than its worth, is in itself unjust and unlawful.'[1] When two contracting parties make an exchange through the medium of money, the price is the expression of the exchange value in money. 'The just price expresses the equivalence, which is the foundation of contractual justice.'[2]

The conception of the just price, though based on Aristotelian conceptions of justice, is essentially Christian. The Roman law had allowed the utmost freedom of contract in sales ; apart from fraud, the two contracting parties were at complete liberty to fix a price at their own risk ; and selfishness was assumed and allowed to be the animating motive of every contracting party. The one limitation to this sweeping rule was in favour of the seller. By a rescript of Diocletian

---

[1] This opinion was accepted by all the later writers, *e.g.* Gerson, *De Cont.*, ii. 5; Biel, *op. cit.*, iv. xv. 10 : 'Si pretium excedit quantitatem valoris rei, vel e converso tolleretur equalitas, erit contractus iniquus.'

[2] Desbuquois, 'La Justice dans l'Echange,' *Semaine Sociale de France*, 1911, p. 167. Gerson says : 'Contractus species est justitiae commutativae quae respicit aequalitatem rei quae venditur ad rem quae emitur, ut servetur aequalitas justi pretii ; propter quam aequalitatem facilius observandum inventa est moneta, vel numisma, vel pecunia,' *De Cont.*, ii. 5.

and Maximian it was enacted that, if a thing were
sold for less than half its value, the seller could
recover the property, unless the buyer chose to
make up the price to the full amount. Although
this rescript was perfectly general in its terms,
some authors contended that it applied only to
sales of land, because the example given was
the sale of a farm.[1] However, the rescript was
quoted by the Fathers as showing that even the
Roman law considered that contracts might be
questioned on equitable grounds in certain cases.[2]
The distinctively Christian notion of just price
seems to have its origin in a passage of St. Augustine ;[3] but the notion was not placed on a philosophical foundation until the thirteenth century.
Even Aquinas, however, although he treats of the
just price at some length, and expresses clear
and categorical opinions upon many points connected with it, does not state the principles on
which the just price itself should be arrived at.
This omission is due, not to the fact that Aquinas
was unfamiliar with these principles, but to the
fact that he took them for granted as they were
not disputed or doubted.[4] We have consequently to look for enlightenment upon this point
in writings other than those of Aquinas. The
subject can be most satisfactorily understood if

[1] Hunter, *Roman Law*, p. 492.

[2] Ashley, *op. cit.*, p. 133.

[3] ' Scio ipse hominem quum venalis codex ei fuisset oblatus, pretiique
ejus ignarum ideo quiddam exiguum poscentem cerneret venditorem,
justum pretium, quod multo amplius erat nec opinanti dedisse ' (*De
Trin.*, xiii. 3).

[4] Palgrave, *Dictionary of Political Economy*, tit. ' Justum Pretium.'

we divide its treatment into two parts: first, a consideration of what constituted the just price in the sale of an article, the price of which was fixed by law; and second, a consideration of what constituted the just price of an article, the price of which was not so fixed.

§ 2. *The Just Price when Price fixed by Law*

Regarding the power of the State to fix prices, the theologians and jurists were in complete agreement. According to Gerson : ' The law may justly fix the price of things which are sold, both movable and immovable, in the nature of rents and not in the nature of rents, and feudal and non-feudal, below which price the seller must not give, or above which the buyer must not demand, however they may desire to do so. As therefore the price is a kind of measure of the equality to be observed in contracts, and as it is sometimes difficult to find that measure with exactitude, on account of the varied and corrupt desires of man, it becomes expedient that the medium should be fixed according to the judgment of some wise man. . . . In the civil state, however, nobody is to be decreed wiser than the lawgiving authority. Therefore it behoves the latter, whenever it is possible to do so, to fix the just price, which may not be exceeded by private consent, and which must be enforced.' . . . [1] Biel practically paraphrases this passage of Gerson, and contends that it is the duty of the prince

[1] *De Cont.*, i. 19.

to fix prices, mainly on account of the difficulty which private contractors find in doing so.[1]

The rules which we find laid down for the guidance of the prince in fixing prices are very interesting, as they show that the mediæval writers had a clear idea of the constituent elements of value. Langenstein, whose famous work on contracts was considered of high authority by later writers, says that the prince should take account of the condition of the place for which the price was to be fixed, the circumstances of the time, the condition of the mass of the people. The different kinds of need which may be felt for goods must also be considered, *indigentiæ naturæ, status, voluptatis,* and *cupiditatis*; and a distinction drawn between extensive and intensive need—the former is greater ' quanto plures re aliqua indigent,' the latter ' quanto minus de illa re habetur.' The general rule is that the prince must seek to find a medium between a price so low as to render labourers, artisans, and merchants unable to maintain themselves suitably, and one so high as to disable the poor from obtaining the necessaries of life. When in doubt, Langenstein concludes, the price should err on the low rather than the high side.[2] Biel gives similar rules : The legislator must regard the needs of man, the abundance or scarcity of things, the difficulty, labour, and risks of production. When all these things are carefully considered the legislator is in a position to fix a just price.[3]

---

[1] *Op. cit.,* IV. xv. 11.   [2] Roscher, *Geschichte,* p. 19.
[3] *Op. cit.,* IV. xv. 10.

According to Endemann, the labour of production, the cost and risk of transport, and the condition of the markets had all to be kept in mind when a fair price was being fixed.[1] We may mention in passing that the power of fixing the just price might be delegated ; prices were frequently fixed by the town authorities, the guilds, and the Church.[2]

The passage from Gerson which we quoted above shows that, when a just price had been fixed by the competent authority, the parties to a contract were bound to keep to it. In other words, the *pretium legitimum* was *ipso facto* the *justum pretium.* On this point there is complete agreement among the writers of the period. Caepolla says, ' When the price is fixed by law or statute, that is the just price, and nobody can receive anything, however small, in excess of it, because the law must be observed ' ;[3] and Biel, ' When a price has been fixed, the contracting parties have sufficient certainty about the equality of value and the justice of the price.'[4] Cossa draws attention to the necessity of the fixed price corresponding with the real price in order that it should maintain its validity. ' The schoolmen talk of the legitimate and irreducible price of a thing which was fixed by authority, and was for obvious reasons of special importance in the case of the necessaries of life. . . . The legitimate price of a

[1] *Studien,* vol. ii. p. 43.

[2] Endemann, *Studien,* vol. i. p. 40 ; Roscher, *Political Economy,* s. 114.

[3] *De Contractibus Simulatis,* 69.   [4] *Op. cit.,* iv. xv. 10.

thing as fixed by authority had to be based upon the natural price, and therefore lost its validity and became a dead letter the moment any change of circumstances made it unfair.' [1]

§ 3. The Just Price when Price not fixed by Law

When the just price was not fixed by any outside authority, the buyer and seller had to arrive at it themselves. The problem before them was to equalise their respective burdens, so that there would be equality of burden between them, or, in other words, to reduce the value of the article sold to terms of money. In order that we may understand how this equality was arrived at, it is important to know the factors which were held to enter into the determination of value.

The first thing upon which the mediæval teachers insist is that value is not determined by the intrinsic excellence of the thing itself, because, if it were, a fly would be more valuable than a pearl, as being intrinsically more excellent.[2] Nor is the value to be measured by the mere utility of the object for satisfying the material needs of man, for in that case, corn should be worth more than precious stones.[3] The value of an object is to be measured by its capacity for satisfying men's wants. ' Valor rerum aestimatur secundum

---

[1] Op. cit., p. 143.

[2] 'In justitia commutativa non estimatur pretium commutabilium secundum naturalem valorem ipsorum, sic enim musca plus valeret quam totus aurum mundi' (Buridan, op. cit. v. 14).

[3] Slater, 'Value in Theology and Political Economy,' Irish Ecclesiastical Record, Sept. 1901.

humanam indigentiam. . . . Dicendum est quod
indigentia humana est mensura naturalis commutabilium ; quod probatur sic : bonitas sive
valor rei attenditur ex fine propter quem exhi-
betur : unde commentator secundo Metaphy-
sicae *nihil est bonum nisi propter causas finales* ;
sed finis naturalis ad quem justitia commutativa
ordinet exteriora commutabilia est supplementum
indigentiae humanae . . . ; igitur supplementum
indigentiae humanae est vera mensura commutabilium. Sed supplementum videtur men-
surari per indigentiam ; majoris enim valoris est
supplementum quod majorem supplet indigentiam.
. . . Item hoc probatur signo, quia videmus quod
illo tempore quo vina deficiunt quia magis indi-
geremus eis ipsa fiunt cariora. . . .[1]

The capacity of an object for satisfying man's
needs could not be measured by its capacity for
satisfying the needs of this or that individual,
but by its capacity for satisfying the needs of the
average member of the community.[2] The Abbé
Desbuquois, in the article from which we have
already quoted, finds in this elevation of the
common estimation an illustration of the general
principle of the mediævals, which we have seen
at work in their teaching on the use of property,

[1] Buridan, *op. cit.*, v. 14 and 16. Antoninus of Florence says that
value is determined by three factors, *virtuositas, raritas,* and *placi-
bilitas (Summa,* ii. 1, 16.)

[2] ' Indigentia istius hominis vel illius non mensurat valorem commutabilium ; sed indigentia communis eorum qui inter se commutare
possunt,' Buridan, *op. cit.,* v. 16. 'Prout communiter venditur
in foro,' Henri de Gand, *Quod Lib.,* xiv. 14 ; Nider, *De Cont.
Merc.,* ii. 1.

that the individual benefit must always be sub-
ordinated to the general welfare. According to
him, it is but one application of the duty of using
one's goods for the common good. ' In the same
way, in allowing the right of exchange—a right,
let us remark in passing, which is but an application of the right of property—and in allowing it
as a means of life necessary to everybody, nature
does not lose sight of the universal destination
of economic goods. One conceives then that the
variations of exchange are not permitted to be
left to the arbitrary judgment of a single man, nor
to be affected by the whims and abuses of individuals ; that value is defined in view of the
general good. The exchange value, as it is in the
general or social order, proceeds from the judgment of the social environment (*milieu social*).' [1]
The writers of the Middle Ages show a very
keen perception of the elements which invest an
object with the value which is accorded to it by
the general estimation. In Aquinas we find
certain elements recognised—'diversitas loci vel
temporis, labor, raritas'—but it is not until the
authors of the fourteenth and fifteenth centuries
that we find a systematic treatment of value.[2]
First and foremost there is the cost of production
of the article, especially the wages of all those
who helped to produce it. Langenstein lays down
that every one can determine for himself the just
price of the wares he has to sell by reckoning what
he needs to support himself in the status which

[1] ' La Justice dans l'Echange,' *Semaine Sociale de France*, 1911,
p. 168.   [2] Brants, *op. cit.*, p. 69.

he occupies.[1]   According to the *Catholic Encyclopædia*,[2] the just price of an article included enough
to pay fair wages to the worker—that is, enough to
enable him to maintain the standard of living of
his class. This, though not stated in so many
words by Aquinas, was probably assumed by him
as too obvious to need repetition.[3] ' The cost
of production of manufactured products,' says
Brants, ' is a legitimate constituent element of
value ; it is according to the cost that the producer can properly fix the value of his product
and of his work.' [4]

The cost of the labour of production was,
however, by no means the only factor which was
admitted to enter into the determination of value.
The passage from Gerson dealing with the circumstances to which the prince must have regard
in fixing a price, which we quoted above, shows
quite clearly that many other factors were
recognised as no less important. This appears
with special clearness in the treatise of Langenstein, whose authority on this subject was always
ranked very high.   Bernardine of Siena is careful
to point out that the expense of production is only
one of the factors which influence the value of an
object.[5] Biel explains that, when no price has
been fixed by law, the just price may be arrived

[1] *De Cont.*, quoted by Roscher, *Geschichte*, p. 20.

[2] Tit. ' Political Economy.'

[3] Palgrave, *Dictionary*, tit. ' Justum Pretium.'

[4] Brants, *op. cit.*, p. 202.

[5] ' Res potest plus vel minus valere tribus modis ; primo secundum
suam virtutem ; secondo modo secundum suam caritatem ; tertio modo
secundum suam placibilitatem et affectionem. . . . Primo observat

at by a reference to the cost of the labour of production, and to the state of the market, and the other circumstances which we have seen above the prince was bound to have regard to in fixing a price. He also allows the price to be raised on account of any anxiety which the production of the goods occasioned him, or any danger he incurred.[1]

It will be apparent from the whole trend of the above that, whereas the remuneration of the labour of all those who were engaged in the production of an article, was one of the elements to be taken into account in reckoning its value, and consequently its just price, it was by no means the only element. Certain so-called Christian socialists have endeavoured to find in the writings of the scholastics support for the Marxian position that all value arises from labour.[2] This endeavour is, however, destined to failure ; we shall see in a later chapter that many forms of unearned income were tolerated and approved by the scholastics ; but all that is necessary here is to draw the attention of the reader to the passages on value to which we have referred. One of the most prominent exponents of the untenable view that the mediævals traced all value to labour is

---

quemdam naturalem ordinem utilium rerum, secundo observat quemdam communem cursum copiaè et inopiae, tertio observat periculum et industriam rerum seu obsequiorum ' (Funk, *Zins und Wucher*, p. 153).

[1] ' Sollicitudo et periculum,' *op. cit.*, IV. xv. 10.

[2] Even Ashley states that ' the doctrine had thus a close resemblance to that of modern Socialists ; labour it regarded both as the sole (human) cause of wealth, and also as the only just claim to the possession of wealth ' (*op. cit.*, vol. i. part ii. p. 393).

the Abbé Hohoff, whose argument that there was
a divorce between value and just price in the
scholastic writings, is ably controverted by Rambaud, who remarks that nobody would have been
more surprised than Aquinas himself at the suggestion that he was the forerunner of Karl Marx.[1]
The idea that the scholastics traced all value to
the labour expended on production is rejected by
many of the most prominent writers on mediæval economic theory. Roscher draws particular
attention to the fact that the canonist teaching
assigned the correct proportions in production to
land, capital, and labour, in contrast to all the
later schools of economists, who have exaggerated
the importance of one or the other of these factors.[2]
Even Knies, who was the first modern writer to
insist on the importance of the cost of production
as an element of value, states that the Church
sought to fix the price of goods in accordance
with the cost of production (*Herstellungskosten*)
and the consumption value (*Gebrauchswerte*).[3]
Brants takes the same view. ' The expenses of
production are in practice the norm of the fixing
of the sale price in the great majority of cases,
above all in a very narrow market, where competition is limited ; moreover, they can, for reasons
of public order, form the basis of a fixing that will
protect the producer and the consumer against the
disastrous consequences of constant oscillations.
The vendor can in principle be remunerated for his

[1] *Op. cit.*, p. 50.   [2] *Political Economy*, s. 48.
[3] *Politische Oekonomie vom Standpuncte der geschichtlichen Methode*,
p. 116.

trouble. It is well that he should be so remunerated ; it is socially useful, and is used as a basis
for fixing price ; but it cannot in any way be said
that this forms the *objective measure of value*, but
that the work and expense are a sufficient title
of remuneration for the fixing of the just price of
the sale of a thing. Some writers have tried to
conclude from this that the authors of the Middle
Ages saw in labour the measure of value. This
conclusion is exaggerated. We may fully admit
that this element enters into the sale price ; but
it is in no way the general measure of value. . . .
The expenses of production constitute, then, *one*
of the legitimate elements of just price ; they are
not the *measure* of value, but a factor often influencing its determination.' [1] ' Labour,' according
to Dr. Cronin, ' is one of the most important of
all the determinants of value, for labour is the
chief element in cost of production, and cost of
production is one of the chief elements in determining the level at which it is useful to buy or sell.
But labour is not the only determinant of value ;
there is, *e.g.*, the price of the raw materials, a price
that is not wholly determined by the labour of
producing those materials.' [2]

The just price, then, in the absence of a legal
fixing, was held to be the price that was in accordance with the *communis estimatio*. Of course,
this did not mean that a plebiscite had to be taken
before every sale, but that any price that was in
accordance with the general course of dealing at
the time and place of the sale was considered

[1] *Op. cit.*, p. 112.   [2] *Ethics*, vol. ii. p. 181.

substantially fair. 'A thing is worth what it
can generally be sold for—at the time of the
contract ; this means what it can be sold for
generally either on that day or the preceding or
following day. One must look to the price at
which similar things are generally sold in the open
market.' ¹ 'We must state precisely,' says the
Abbé Desbuquois, ' the character of this common
estimation ; it did not mean the universal
suffrage ; although it expresses the universal
interest, it proceeds in practice from the evalua-
tion of competent men, taken in the social environment where the exchange value operates.
If one supposes a sovereign tribunal of arbitration
where all the rights of all the weak and all the
strong economic factors are taken into account,
the just price appears as the sentence or decision
of this court.' ² 'For the scholastics, the common estimation meant an ethical judgment of at
least the most influential members of the community, anticipating the markets and fixing the
rate of exchange.' ³

It is quite incorrect to say, as has been sometimes said, that the mediæval just price was in
no way different from the competition price of
to-day which is arrived at by the higgling of the
market. Dr. Cunningham is very explicit and
clear on this point. ' Common estimation is thus
the exponent of the natural or normal or just
price according to either the mediæval or modern
view ; but, whereas we rely on the higgling of the

¹ Caepolla, De Cont. Sim., 72.   ² Op. cit., pp. 169-70.
³ Fr. Kelleher in the Irish Theological Quarterly, vol. xi. p. 133.

market as the means of bringing out what is the common estimate of any object, mediæval economists believed that it was possible to bring common estimation into operation beforehand, and by the consultation of experts to calculate out what was the just price. If common estimation was thus organised, either by the town authorities or guilds or parliament, it was possible to determine beforehand what the price should be and to lay down a rule to this effect ; in modern times we can only look back on the competition prices and say by reflection what the common estimation has been.'[1] 'The common estimation of which the Canonists spoke,' says Dr. Ryan, ' was conscious social judgment that fixed price beforehand, and was expressed chiefly in custom, while the social estimate of to-day is in reality an unconscious resultant of the higgling of the market, and finds its expression only in market price.'[2] The phrase 'res tanti valet quanti vendi potest,' which is so often used to prove that the mediæval doctors permitted full competitive prices in the modern sense, must be understood to mean that a thing could be sold at any figure which was within the limits of the minimum and maximum just price.[3]

The last sentence suggests that the just price was not a fixed and unalterable standard, but was somewhat wide and elastic. On this all writers are agreed. 'The just price of things,' says Aquinas, ' is not fixed with mathematical pre-

[1] *Growth of English Industry and Commerce*, vol. i. p. 353.
[2] *Living Wage*, p. 28.   [3] Lessius, *De Justitia et Jure*, xxi. 19.

cision, but depends on a kind of estimate, so that
a slight addition or subtraction would not seem
to destroy the equality of justice,'¹ Caepolla
repeats this dictum, with the reservation that,
when the just price is fixed by law, it must be
rigorously observed.² ' Note,' says Gerson, ' that
the equality of commutative justice is not exact
or unchangeable, but has a good deal of latitude,
within the bounds of which a greater or less price
may be given without justice being infringed ; '³
and Biel insists on the same latitude, from which
he draws the conclusion that the just price is
constantly varying from day to day and from
place to place.⁴ Generally it was said that there
was a maximum, medium, and minimum just
price ; and that any price between the maximum
and minimum was valid, although the medium
was to be aimed at as far as possible.

The price fixed by common estimation was
therefore the one to be observed in most cases,
and it was at all times a safe guide to follow.
If, however, the parties either knew or had good
reason to believe that the common estimation
had fixed the price wrongly, they were not bound
to follow it, but should arrive at a just price themselves, having regard to the various considerations
given above.⁵

It did not make any difference whether the

¹ II. ii. 77, 1, ad. 1.   ² De Cont. Sim., 58.
³ De Cont., ii. 11.   ⁴ Op. cit., IV. xv. 10.
⁵ Nider, De Cont. Merc. ii. : ' Si vero scit vel credit communitatem
errare in estimatione pretii rei ; tunc nullo modo debet eam sequi ;
quia etiam si reciperet verum et justum pretium, tamen faceret contra
conscientiam.'

price was paid immediately or at some future
date. To increase the price in return for the
giving of credit was not allowed, as it was deemed
usurious—as indeed it was. It was held that the
seller, in not taking his money immediately, was
simply making a loan of that amount to the
buyer, and that to receive anything more than
the sum lent would be usury. Aquinas is quite
clear on this point. 'If a man wish to sell his
goods at a higher price than that which is just, so
that he may wait for the buyer to pay, it is mani-
festly a case of usury ; because this waiting for
the payment of the price has the character of a
loan, so that whatever he demands beyond the
just price in consideration of this delay, is like a
price for a loan, which pertains to usury. In
like manner, if a buyer wishes to buy goods at a
lower price than what is just, for the reason that
he pays for the goods before they can be delivered,
it is likewise a sin of usury ; because again this
anticipated payment of money has the character
of a loan, the price of which is the rebate on the
just price of the goods sold. On the other hand,
if a man wishes to allow a rebate on the just price
in order that he may have his money sooner, he is
not guilty of the sin of usury.' [1] If, however, the
seller, by giving credit, suffered any damage, he
was entitled to be recompensed ; this, as we shall
see, was an ordinary feature of usury law. It
could not be said that the price was raised. The
price remained the same ; but the seller was
entitled to something further than the price by

[1] II. ii. 78, 2, ad. 7. See *Decret. Greg.*, v. 19, *de usuris*, cc. 6 and 10.

way of damages.[1] It was by the application of this principle that a seller was justified in demanding more than the current price for an article which possessed some individual or sentimental value for him. ' In such a case the just price will depend not only on the thing sold, but on the loss which the sale brings on the seller. . . . No man should sell what is not his, though he may charge for the loss he suffers.' [2] On the other hand, it was strictly forbidden to raise the price on account of the individual need of the buyer.[3]

§ 4. *The Just Price of Labour*

Particular rules were laid down for determining the just price of certain classes of goods. These need not be treated in detail, as they were merely applications of the general principle to particular cases, and whatever interest they possess is in the domain of practice rather than of theory. In the sale of immovable property the rule was that the value should be arrived at by a consideration of the annual fruits of the property.[4] The only one of the particular contracts which need detain us here is that of a contract of service for wages (*locatio operarum*). Wages were considered as ruled by the laws relating to just price. ' That is called a wage (*merces*) which is paid to any one as a recompense for his work and labour. Therefore, as it is an act of justice to give a just price

[1] Endemann, *Studien*, vol. ii. pp. 49 ; Desbuquois, *op. cit.*, p. 174.
[2] II. ii. 77, 1.   [3] *Ibid.*
[4] Caepolla, *de Cont. Sim.*, 78 ; Carletus, *Summa Angelica*, lxv.

for a thing taken from another person, so also to
pay the wages of work and labour is an act of
justice.' [1] Again, ' Remuneration of service or
work . . . can be priced at a money value, as
may be seen in the case of those who offer for hire
the labour which they exercise by work or by
tongue.' [2] Biel insists that the value of labour
is subject to the same influences as the value of
any other commodity which is offered for sale,
and that therefore a just price must be observed
in buying it. [3]

This, according to Brants, [4] is essentially a matter
upon which more enlightenment will be found in
histories of the working classes [5] than in books
dealing with the enunciation of abstract theories ;
nevertheless, it is possible to state generally that
it was regarded as the duty of employers to give
such a wage as would support the worker in accordance with the requirements of his class. In the
great majority of cases the rate of wages was
fixed by some public—municipal or corporative
—authority, but Langenstein enunciates a rule
which seems to approach the statement of a general
theory. According to him, when a man has

[1] Aquinas, *Summa*, II. ii. 114, 1.   [2] II. ii. 78, 2, ad. 3.
[3] *Op. cit.*, IV. xv. 10. Modern Socialists caricature the correct
principle ' that labour is a commodity ' into ' the labourer is a commodity '—a great difference, which is not sufficiently understood by
many present-day writers. (See Roscher, *Political Economy*, s. 160.)
[4] *Op. cit.*, p. 103.
[5] An excellent bibliography of books dealing with the history of the
working classes in the Middle Ages is to be found in Brants, *op. cit.*,
p. 105. The need for examining concrete economic phenomena is
insisted on in Ryan's *Living Wage*, p. 28.

something to sell, and has no indication of the just price from its being fixed by any outside authority, he must endeavour to get such a price as will *reasonably* recompense him for any outlay he may have incurred, and will enable him to provide for his needs, spiritual and temporal.[1] It was not until the sixteenth century that the fixing of the just price of wages was submitted to scientific discussion;[2] in the fourteenth and fifteenth centuries there is little to be found bearing on this subject except the passage of Langenstein which we have quoted, and some strong exhortations by Antoninus of Florence to masters to pay good wages.[3] The reason for this paucity of authority upon a subject of so much importance is that in practice the machinery provided by the guilds had the effect of preserving a substantially just remuneration to the artisan. When a man is in perfect health he does not bother to read medical books. In the same way, the proper remuneration of labour was so universally recognised as a duty, and so satisfactorily enforced, that it seems to have been taken for granted, and therefore passed over, by the

[1] *De Cont.* We have here a recognition of the principle that the value of labour is not to be measured by anything extrinsic to itself, *e.g.* by the value of the product, but by its own natural function and end, and this function and end is the supplying of the requirements of human life. The wage must, therefore, be capable of supplying the same needs that the expenditure of a labourer's energy is meant to supply. (See Cronin, *Ethics*, vol. ii. p. 390.)

[2] Brants, *op. cit.*, p. 118.

[3] The passages from the *Summa* of Antoninus bearing on the subject are reprinted in Brants, *op. cit.*, p. 120.

writers of the period. One may agree with Brants in concluding that, ' the principle of just price in sales was applied to wages ; fluctuations in wages were not allowed ; the just price, as in sales, rested on the approximate equality of the services rendered; and that this equality was estimated by common opinion.' [1] Of course, in the case of slave labour it could not be said that any wage was paid. The master was entitled to the services of the slave, and in return was bound to furnish him with the necessaries of life.[2]

§ 5. *Value of the Conception of the Just Price*

It is probably correct to say that the canonical teaching on just price was negative rather than positive ; in other words, that it did not so much aim at positively fixing the price at which goods should be sold, as negatively at indicating the practices in buying and selling which were unjust. ' The doctrine of just price,' according to Dr. Ryan, ' may sometimes have been associated with incorrect views of industrial life, but all competent authorities agree that it was a fairly sound attempt to define the equities of mediæval exchanges, and that it was tolerably successful in practice.' [3] The condition of mediæval markets was frequently such that the competition was not really fair competition, and consequently the price arrived at by competition would be unfair

---

[1] *Op. cit.*, p. 125.

[2] Brants, *op. cit.*, p. 116, quoting *Le Livre du Trésor* of Brunetto Latini.   [3] *The Living Wage*, p. 27.

either to buyer or seller. ' This,' according to
Dr. Cunningham, ' was the very thing which
mediæval regulation had been intended to prevent, as any attempt to make gain out of the
necessities of others, or to reap profit from un-
looked-for occurrences would have been condemned as extortion. It is by taking advantage
of such fluctuations that money is most frequently
made in modern times ; but the whole scheme of
commercial life in the Middle Ages was supposed
to allow of a regular profit on each transaction.'[1]
There might be some doubt as to the positive
justice of this or that price ; but there could be no
doubt as to the injustice of a price which was
enhanced by the necessities of the poor, or the
engrossing of a vital commodity.[2] Merely to buy
up the whole supply of a certain commodity,
even if it were bought up by a ' ring ' of merchants,
provided that the commodity was resold within
the limits of the just price, was not a sin against
justice, though it might be a sin against charity.[3]
If the authorities granted a monopoly, they must
at the same time fix a just price.[4] A monopoly
which was not privileged by the State, and which
had for its aim the raising of the price of goods
above the just price was regarded with universal
reprobation.[5] ' Whoever buys up corn, meat,
and wine,' says Trithemius, ' in order to drive
up their price and to amass money at the cost of

[1] *Growth of English Industry and Commerce*, vol. i. p. 460.
[2] Endemann, *Studien*, vol. ii. p. 60.
[3] Lessius, *De Justitia et Jure*, II. xx. 1, 21.   [4] *Ibid.*
[5] Langenstein, *De Cont.* ; Biel, *op. cit.*, IV. xv. 11.

others is, according to the laws of the Church,
no better than a common criminal. In a well-
governed community all arbitrary raising of prices
in the case of articles of food and clothing is per-
emptorily stopped ; in times of scarcity merchants
who have supplies of such commodities can be
compelled to sell them at fair prices ; for in every
community care should be taken that all the
members should be provided for, and not only a
small number be allowed to grow rich, and revel
in luxury to the hurt and prejudice of the many.[1]
Thus the doctrine of the just price was a deadly
weapon with which to fight the 'profiteer.' The
engrosser was looked upon as the natural enemy
of the poor ; and the power of the trading class
was justly reckoned so great, that in cases of doubt
prices were always fixed low rather than high.
In other words, the buyer—that is to say, the
community—was the subject of protection rather
than the seller.[2]

It must at the same time be clearly kept in
mind that the seller was also protected. All the
authorities are unanimous that it was as sinful
for the buyer to give too little as for the seller to
demand too much, and it is this aspect of the just
price which appears most favourable in comparison
with the theory of price of the classical economists.
In the former case prices were fixed having regard
to the wages necessary for the producer ; in the
latter the wages of the producer are determined
by the price at which he can sell his goods, exposed

[1] Quoted in Janssen, *op. cit.*, vol. ii. p. 102.
[2] Roscher, *Geschichte*, p. 12.

to the competition of machinery or foreign—possibly slave—labour.[1] According to the *Catholic Encyclopædia* : ' To the mediæval theologian the just price of an article included enough to pay fair wages to the worker—that is, enough to enable him to maintain the standard of living of his class.' [2] ' The difference,' says Dr. Cunningham, ' which emerges according as we start from one principle or the other comes out most distinctly with reference to wages. In the Middle Ages wages were taken as a first charge ; in modern times the reward of the labourer cannot but fluctuate in connection with fluctuations in the utility and market price of the things. There must always be a connection between wages and prices, but in the olden times wages were the first charge, and prices on the whole depended on them, while in modern times wages are, on the other hand, directly affected by prices.' [3] Dr. Cunningham draws attention to the fact that the labouring classes rejected the idea of the fixing of a just price for their services when, from a variety of causes, a situation arose when they were able to earn by open competition a reward higher than what was necessary to support them according to their state in life.[4] Nowadays the reverse has taken place ; unrestricted competition has in many cases resulted in the reduction of wages to a level below the margin of subsistence ; and the

---

[1] Ashley, *op. cit.*, vol. i. pt. i. p. 129.
[2] Art. ' Political Economy.'
[3] *Growth of English Industry and Commerce*, vol. i. p. 461.
[4] *Christianity and Economic Science*, p. 29.

general cry of the working classes is for the compulsory fixing of minimum rates of wages which will ensure that their subsistence will not be liable to be impaired by the fluctuations of the markets. What the workers of the present day look to as a desirable, but almost unattainable, ideal, was the universal practice in the ages when economic relations were controlled by Christian principles.

§ 6. *Was the Just Price Subjective or Objective?*

The question whether the just price was essentially subjective or objective has recently formed the subject matter of an interesting and ably conducted discussion, provoked by certain remarks in Dr. Cunningham's *Western Civilisation.*[1] Dr. Cunningham, although admiring the ethical spirit which animated the conception of the just price, thought at the same time that the economic ideas underlying the conception were so undeveloped and unsound that the theory could not be applied in practice at the present day. ' Their economic analysis was very defective, and the theory of price which they put forward was untenable; but the ethical standpoint which they took is well worth examination, and the practical measures which they recommended appear to have been highly beneficial in the circumstances in which they had to deal. Their actions were not unwise; their common-sense morality was sound; but the economic theories by which they tried to

[1] Pp. 77-9.

give an intellectual justification for their rules
and their practice were quite erroneous. . . .
The attempt to determine an ideal price implies
that there can and ought to be stability in relative
values and stability in the measure of values—
which is absurd. The mediæval doctrine and its
application rested upon another assumption which
we have outlived. Value is not a quality which
inheres in an object so that it can have the same
worth for everybody ; it arises from the personal
preference and needs of different people, some of
whom desire a thing more and some less, some
of whom want to use it in one way and some in
another. Value is not objective—intrinsic in the
object—but subjective, varying with the desire
and intentions of the possessors or would-be
possessors ; and, because it is thus subjective,
there cannot be a definite ideal value which every
article ought to possess, and still more a just price
as the measure of that ideal value.' In these
and similar observations to be found in the *Growth
of English History and Commerce*, Dr. Cunningham
showed that he profoundly misunderstood the
doctrine of the just price ; the objectivity which
he attributed to it was not the objectivity ascribed
to it by the scholastics. It was to correct this
misunderstanding that Father Slater contributed
an article to the *Irish Theological Quarterly* [1]
pointing out that the just price was subjective
rather than objective. This article, which was
afterwards reprinted in *Some Aspects of Moral
Theology*, and the conclusions of which were

[1] Vol. iv. p. 146.

embodied in the same writer's work on Moral
Theology, was controverted in a series of articles
by Father Kelleher in the *Irish Theological
Quarterly*.[1]
Father Slater draws attention to the fact that
Dr. Cunningham overlooked to some extent the
importance of common estimation in arriving at
the just price. He points out that, far from
objects being invested with some immutable objective value, their value was in fact determined
by the price which the community as a whole was
willing to pay for them: 'As the value in exchange will be determined by what the members
of the community at the time are prepared to
give, . . . it will be determined by the social
estimation of its utility for the support of life and
its scarcity. It will depend upon its capacity to
satisfy the wants and desires of the people with
whom commercial transactions are possible and
practicable. Father Slater then goes on categorically to refute Dr. Cunningham's presentation
of the objectivity of price: 'All that that doctrine asserts is that there should be, and that
there is, an equivalent in social value between
the commodity and its price at a certain time
and in a certain place ; it says nothing whatever
about the stability or permanence of prices at
different times and at different places. By maintaining that the just price did not depend upon
the valuation of the individual buyer or seller
the mediæval doctors did not dream of making

[1] 'Market Prices,' vol. ix. p. 398 and vol. x. p. 163 ; and 'Father
Slater on Just Price and Value,' vol. xi. p. 159.

it intrinsic to the object.' In the work on Moral
Theology, to which we have referred, expressions
occur which lead one to believe that Father Slater
did not see any great difference between the
mediæval just price arrived at by common estimation and the modern normal or market price
arrived at by open competition. Thus, in endeavouring to correct Dr. Cunningham's misunderstanding, Father Slater seems to have gone
too far in the other direction, and his position has
been ably and, in our judgment, successfully,
controverted by Father Kelleher.

The point at issue between the upholders of the
two opposing views on just price is well stated by
Father Kelleher in the first of his articles on the
subject : 'We must try to find out whether the
just and fair price determined the rate of exchange,
or whether the rate of exchange, being determined
without an objective standard and merely according to the play of human motives, determines
what we call the just and fair price.' [1] We have
already demonstrated that the common estimation referred to by the mediæval doctors was something quite apart from the modern higgling in
the market ; and that, far from being merely the
result of unbridled competition on both sides, it
was rather the considered judgment of the best-
informed members of the community. As we
have seen, even Dr. Cunningham admits that
there was a fundamental difference between the
common estimation of the scholastics and the
modern competitive price. This is clearly demon-

[1] *Irish Theological Quarterly*, vol. ix. p. 41.

strated by Father Kelleher, who further estab-
lishes the proposition that the modern price is
purely subjective, and that no subjective price can
rest on an ethical basis. The question at issue
therefore between what we may call the subjective
and objective schools is not whether the sale price
was determined by competition in the modern
sense, but whether the common estimation of
those best qualified to form an opinion on the
subject in itself determined the just price, or
whether it was merely the most reliable evidence
of what the just price in fact was at a particular
moment.

Father Kelleher draws attention to the fact
that Aquinas in his article on price did not specifically affirm that the just price was objective, but
he explains this omission by saying that the
objectivity of the price was so well and universally
understood that it was unnecessary expressly to
restate it. Indeed, as we saw above, the teaching
of Aquinas on price left a great deal to be supplied
by later writers, not because he was in any doubt
about the subject, but because the theory was so
well understood. 'Not even in St. Thomas can
we find a formal discussion of the moral obligation
of observing an objective equivalence in contracts
of buying and selling. He simply took it for
granted, as, indeed, was inevitable, seeing that, up
to his time and for long after, all Catholic thought
and legislation proceeded on that hypothesis.
But that he actually did take it for granted, he
has given many clear indications in his article on
Justice which leave us no room for reasonable

doubt.'[1]   As Father Kelleher very cogently
points out, the discussion in Aquinas's article on
commerce, whether it was lawful to buy cheap and
sell dear, very clearly indicates that the author
maintained the objective theory, because if the
just price were simply determined by what people
were willing to give, this question could not have
arisen.

Nor is the fact that the just price admitted of a
certain elasticity an argument in favour of its
being subjective. Father Kelleher fully admits
that the common estimation was the general
criterion of just price, and, of course, the common
estimation could not, of its very nature, be rigid
and immutable. ' Commodities should, indeed,
exchange according to their objective value, but,
even so, commodities could not carry their value
stamped on their faces.   Even if we assume that
the standard of exchange was the cost of production, there would still remain room for a certain
amount of difference of opinion as to what exactly
their value would be in particular instances.
Suppose that the commodity offered for sale was
a suit of clothes, in estimating its value on the basis
of the cost of production, opinions might differ as
to the precise amount of time required for making
it, or as to the cost of the cloth out of which it was
made.   Unless recourse was to be had to an almost
interminable process of calculations, nobody could
say authoritatively what precisely the value was,
and in practice the determination of value had
perforce to be left to the ordinary human estimate

of what it was, which of its very nature was bound
to admit a certain margin of fluctuation. Thus
we can easily understand how, even with an
objective standard of value, the just price might
be admitted to vary within the limits of the
maximum as it might be expected to be estimated by sellers and the minimum as it would
appear just to buyers. The sort of estimation
of which St. Thomas speaks is therefore nothing
else than a judgment, which, being human, is
liable to be slightly in excess or defect of the
objective value about which it is formed.'[1] As
Father Kelleher puts it on a later page, ' There is
a sense certainly in which, with a solitary exception in the case of wages, it may be said with
perfect truth that the common estimation determines the just price. That is, the common estimation is the proximate practical criterion.'[2]

Father Kelleher uses in support of his contention a very ingenious argument drawn from the
doctrine of usury. As we said in the first chapter,
and as we shall prove in detail in the next section,
the prohibition of usury was simply one of the
applications of the theory of equivalence in contracts—in other words, it was the determination of
the just price to be paid in an exchange of money
for money. If, asks Father Kelleher, the common
estimation was the final test of just price, why was
not moderate usury allowed ? That the general
opinion of the community in the Middle Ages was
undoubtedly in favour of allowing a reasonable
percentage on loans is shown by the constant

[1] *Irish Theological Quarterly*, vol. x. p. 166.   [2] P. 173.

striving of the Church to prevent such a practice. Nevertheless the Church did not for a moment relax its teaching on usury in spite of the almost universal judgment of the people. Here, therefore, is a clear example of one contract in which the standard of value is clearly objective, and it is only reasonable to draw the conclusion that the same standard which applied in contracts of the exchange of money should apply in contracts of the sale of other articles.

Father Kelleher's contention seems to be completely supported by the passage from Nider which we have cited above, to the effect that the common estimation ceases to be the final test of the just price when the contracting parties know or believe that the common estimation has erred.[1] This seems to us clearly to show that the common estimation was but the most generally received test of what the just price in fact was, but that it was in no sense a final or irrefutable criterion.[2]

The theory that the just price was objective seems to be accepted by the majority of the best modern students of the subject. Sir William Ashley says : ' The fundamental difference between the mediæval and modern point of view is . . . that

[1] *De Cont. Merc.*, II. xv. Nider was regarded as a very weighty authority on the subject of contracts (Endemann, *Studien*, vol. ii. p. 8).

[2] The argument in favour of what we have called the ' objective ' theory of the just price is strengthened by the consideration that goods do not satisfy mere subjective whims, but supply real wants. For example, food supplies a real need of the human being, as also does clothing ; in the one case hunger is appeased, and in the other cold is warded off, just as drugs used in medical practice produce real objective effects on the person taking them.

with us value is something entirely subjective ;
it is what each individual cares to give for a thing.
With Aquinas it was entirely objective ; something outside the will of the individual purchaser
or seller ; something attached to the thing itself,
existing whether he liked it or not, and that he
ought to recognise.' [1] Palgrave's *Dictionary of
Political Economy*, following the authority of Knies,
expresses the same opinion : ' Perhaps the contrast between mediæval and modern ideas of value
is best expressed by saying that with us value is
usually something subjective, consisting of the
mental determination of buyer and seller, while
to the schoolmen it was in a sense objective,
something intrinsically bound up with the commodity itself.' [2] Dr. Ryan agrees with this view :
' The theologians of the sixteenth and seventeenth
centuries assumed that the objective price would
be fair, since it was determined by the social
estimate. In their opinion the social estimate
would embody the requirements of objective
justice as fully as any device or institution that
was practically available. For the condition of
the Middle Ages and the centuries immediately
following, this reasoning was undoubtedly correct.
The agencies which created the social estimate
and determined prices—namely the civil law, the
guilds, and custom—succeeded fairly in establish-
ing a price that was equitable to all concerned.' [3]
Dr. Cleary says : ' True, the *pretium legale* is

[1] *Op. cit.*, vol. i. pt. i. p. 140.   [2] Art. ' Justum Pretium.'
[3] ' The Moral Aspect of Monopoly,' by J. A. Ryan, D.D., *Irish
Theological Quarterly*, iii. p. 275; and see *Distributive Justice*, pp. 332-4.

regarded as being a just price, but in order that it may be just, it supposes some objective basis— in other words, it rather declares than constitutes the just price.'[1] Haney is also strongly of opinion that the just price was objective. 'Briefly stated, the doctrine was that every commodity had some one true value which was objective and absolute.'[2] The greater number of modern students therefore who have given most care and attention to the question are inclined to the opinion that the just price was not subjective, but objective, and we see no valid reason for disagreeing with this view, which seems to be fully warranted by the original authorities.

§ 7. *The Mediæval Attitude towards Commerce*

Before passing from the question of price, we must discuss the legitimacy of the various occupations which were concerned with buying and selling. The principal matter which arises for consideration in this regard is the attitude of the mediæval theologians towards commerce. Aquinas discusses the legitimacy of commerce in the same question in which he discusses just price, and indeed the two subjects are closely allied, because the importance of the observance of justice in buying and selling grew urgent as commerce extended and advanced.

In order to understand the disapprobation with which commerce was on the whole regarded in

[1] *Op. cit.*, p. 193.
[2] *History of Economic Thought*, p. 75.

the Middle Ages, it is necessary to appreciate the
importance of the Christian teaching on the dignity
of labour.   The principle that, far from being a
degrading or humiliating occupation, as it had
been regarded in Greece and Rome, manual labour
was, on the contrary, one of the most noble ways
of serving God, effected a revolution in the economic sphere analogous to that which the Christian
sanctification of marriage effected in the domestic
sphere.   The Christian teaching on labour was
grounded on the Divine precepts contained in
both the Old and New Testaments,[1] and upon
the example of Christ, who was Himself a working man.   The Gospel was preached amongst
the poor, and St. Paul continued his humble
labours during his apostolate.[2]   A life of idleness
was considered something to be avoided, instead
of something to be desired, as it had been in the
ancient civilisations.   Gerson says it is against
the nature of man to wish to live without labour
as usurers do,[3] and Langenstein inveighs against
usurers and all who live without work.[4]   ' We
read in Sebastian Brant that the idlers are the
most foolish amongst fools, they are to every
people like smoke to the eyes or vinegar to the
teeth.   Only by labour is God truly praised and
honoured ; and Trithemius says " Man is born to
labour as the bird to fly, and hence it is contrary

---

[1] Gen. iii. 19; Ps. cxxvii. 2; 2 Thess. iii. 10.   The last-mentioned
text is explained, in opposition to certain Socialist interpretations
which have been put on it, by Dr. Hogan in the *Irish Ecclesiastical
Record*, vol. xxv. p. 45.   [2] Wallon, *op. cit.*, vol. iii. p. 401.
[3] *De Cont.*, i. 13.   [4] *De Cont.*

to the nature of man when he thinks to live without work." ' [1] The example of the monasteries, where the performance of all sorts of manual labour was not thought inconsistent with the administration of the sacred offices and the pursuit of the highest intellectual exercises, acted as a powerful assertion to the laity of the dignity of labour in the scheme of things. [2] The value of the monastic example in this respect cannot be too highly estimated. ' When we consider the results of the founding of monasteries,' says Dr. Cunningham, ' we find influences at work that were plainly economic. These communities can be best understood when we think of them as Christian industrial colonies, and remember that they moulded society rather by example than by precept. We are so familiar with the attacks and satires on monastic life that were current at the Reformation period, that it may seem almost a paradox to say that the chief claim of the monks to our gratitude lies in this, that they helped to diffuse a better appreciation of the duty and dignity of labour.' [3]

The result of this teaching and example was that, in the Middle Ages, labour had been raised to a position of unquestioned dignity. The economic benefit of this attitude towards labour must be obvious. It made the working classes take a direct pride and interest in their work, which was represented to be a means of sanctifi-

[1] Janssen, op. cit., vol. ii. pp. 93-4.
[2] Levasseur, Histoire des Classes ouvrières en France, vol. i. pp. 182 et seq.   [3] Western Civilisation, vol. ii. p. 35.

cation. 'Labour,' according to Dr. Cunningham,
' was said to be pregnant with a double advantage
—the privilege of sharing with God in His work of
carrying out His purpose, and the opportunity of
self-discipline and the helping of one's fellow-men.'[1]
' Industrial work,' says Levasseur, ' in the times
of antiquity had always had, in spite of the institutions of certain Emperors, a degrading character,
because it had its roots in slavery ; after the in-
vasion, the grossness of the barbarians and the
levelling of towns did not help to rehabilitate it.
It was the Church which, in proclaiming that
Christ was the son of a carpenter, and the Apostles
were simple workmen, made known to the world
that work is honourable as well as necessary.
The monks proved this by their example, and thus
helped to give to the working classes a certain
consideration which ancient society had denied
them.   Manual labour became a source of sanctification.'[2]   The high esteem in which labour was
held appears from the whole artistic output of the
Middle Ages. ' Many of the simple artists of the
time represented the saints holding some instrument of work or engaged in some industrial
pursuit ; as, for instance, the Blessed Virgin
spinning as she sat by the cradle of the divine
Infant, and St. Joseph using a saw or carpenter's
tools. " Since the Saints," says the *Christian
Monitor*, " have laboured, so shall the Christian
learn that by honourable labour he can glorify
God, do good, and save his own soul." '[3]   Work

[1] *Christianity and Economic Science*, pp. 26-7.
[2] *Op. cit.*, vol. i. p. 187.   [3] Janssen, *op. cit.*, vol. ii. p. 9.

was, alongside of prayer and inseparable from it, the perfection of Christian life.[1]

It must not be supposed, however, that manual labour alone was thought worthy of praise. On the contrary, the necessity for mental and spiritual workers was fully appreciated, and all kinds of labour were thought equally worthy of honour. ' Heavy labourer's work is the inevitable yoke of punishment, which, according to God's righteous verdict, has been laid upon all the sons of Adam. But many of Adam's descendants seek in all sorts of cunning ways to escape from the yoke and to live in idleness without labour, and at the same time to have a superfluity of useful and necessary things ; some by robbery and plunder, some by usurious dealings, others by lying, deceit, and all the countless forms of dishonest and fraudulent gain, by which men are for ever seeking to get riches and abundance without toil. But while such men are striving to throw off the yoke righteously imposed on them by God, they are heaping on their shoulders a heavy burden of sin. Not so, however, do the reasonable sons of Adam proceed ; but, recognising in sorrow that for the sins of their first father God has righteously ordained that only through the toil of labour shall they obtain what is necessary to life, they take the yoke patiently on them. . . . Some of them, like the peasants, the handicraftsmen, and the tradespeople, procure for themselves and others, in the sweat of their brows and by physical work, the necessary sustenance of life. Others, who

[1] Wallon, *op. cit.*, vol. i. p. 410.

labour in more honourable ways, earn the right
to be maintained by the sweat of others' brows—
for instance, those who stand at the head of the
commonwealth ; for by their laborious exertion
the former are enabled to enjoy the peace, the
security, without which they could not exist.
The same holds good of those who have the charge
of spiritual matters. . . .' [1] ' Because,' says
Aquinas, ' many things are necessary to human
life, with which one man cannot provide himself,
it is necessary that different things should be done
by different people ; therefore some are tillers of
the soil, some are raisers of cattle, some are
builders, and so on ; and, because human life does
not simply mean corporal things, but still more
spiritual things, therefore it is necessary that sóme
people should be released from the care of attend-
ing to temporal matters. This distribution of
different offices amongst different people is in
accordance with Divine providence.' [2]

All forms of labour being therefore admitted to
be honourable and necessary, there was no difficulty felt about justifying their reward. It was
always common ground that services of all kinds
were entitled to be properly remunerated, and
questions of difficulty only arose when a claim was
made for payment in a transaction where the
element of service was not apparent. [3] The different occupations in which men were engaged were
therefore ranked in a well-recognised hierarchy

---

[1] Langenstein, quoted in Janssen, *op. cit.*, p. 95.
[2] *Summa Cont. Gent.*, iii. 134.
[3] Aquinas, *Summa*, II. ii. 77, 4 ; Nider, *op. cit.*, II. x.

of dignity according to the estimate to which they
were held to be entitled.   The Aristotelean division of industry into *artes possessivae* and *artes
pecuniativae* was generally followed, the former
being ranked higher than the latter. ' The in-
dustries called *possessivae*, which are immediately
useful to the individual, to the family, and to
society, producing natural wealth, are also the
most natural as well as the most estimable.   But
all the others should not be despised.   The natural
arts are the true economic arts, but the arts which
produce artificial riches are also estimable in so
far as they serve the true national economy; the
commutation of the exchanges and the *cambium*
being necessary to the general good, are good in so
far as they are subordinate to the end of true
economy.   One may say the same thing about
commerce.   In order, then, to estimate the value
of an industrial art, one must examine its relation to the general good.' [1]   Even the *artes possessivae* were not all considered equally worthy of
praise, but were ranked in a curious order of pro-
fessional hierarchy.   Agriculture was considered
the highest, next manufacture, and lastly commerce.   Roscher says that, whereas all the
scholastics were agreed on the excellence of agriculture as an occupation, the best they could say
of manufacture was *Deo non displicet*, whereas of
commerce they said *Deo placere non potest*; and
draws attention to the interesting consequence of
this, namely, that the various classes of goods that
took part in the different occupations were also

[1] Brants, *op. cit.*, p. 82.

ranked in a certain order of sacredness. Immovables were thought more worthy of protection against execution and distress than movables, and movables than money.[1] Aquinas advises the rulers of States to encourage the *artes possessivae*, especially agriculture.[2] The fullest analysis of the order in which the different *artes possessivae* should be ranked is to be found in Buridan's *Commentaries on Aristotle's Politics.* He places first agriculture, which comprises cattle-breeding, tillage, and hunting ; secondly, manufacture, which helps to supply man's corporal needs, such as building and architecture ; thirdly, administrative occupations; and lastly, commerce. The Christian Exhortation, quoted by Janssen,[3] says, ' The farmer must in all things be protected and encouraged, for all depend on his labour, from the monarch to the humblest of mankind, and his handiwork is in particular honourable and well pleasing to God.'

The division of occupations according to their dignity adopted by Nicholas Oresme is somewhat unusual. He divides professions into (1) honourable, or those which increase the actual quantity of goods in the community or help its development, such as ecclesiastical offices, the law, the soldiery, the peasantry, artisans, and merchants, and (2) degrading—such as *campsores, mercatores monetae seu billonatores.*[4]

---

[1] *Geschichte*, p. 7.
[2] *De Regimine Principum*, vol. ii. chaps. v. and vi.
[3] *Op. cit.*, vol. i. p. 297.
[4] *Tractatus de Origine, etc., Monetarum.*

No occupation, therefore, which involved labour, whether manual or mental, gave any ground for difficulty with regard to its remuneration. The business of the trader or merchant, on the other hand, was one which called for some explanation. It is important to understand what commerce was taken to mean. The definition which Aquinas gives was accepted by all later writers : ' A tradesman is one whose business consists in the exchange of things. According to the philosopher, exchange of things is twofold ; one natural, as it were, and necessary, whereby one commodity is exchanged for another, or money taken in exchange for a commodity in order to satisfy the needs of life. Such trading, properly speaking, does not belong to traders, but rather to housekeepers or civil servants, who have to provide the household or the State with the necessaries of life. The other kind of exchange is either that of money for money, or of any commodity for money, not on account of the necessities of life, but for profit ; and this kind of trade, properly speaking, regards traders.' It is to be remarked in this definition, that it is essential, to constitute trade, that the exchange or sale should be for the sake of profit, and this point is further emphasised in a later passage of the same article : ' Not every one that sells at a higher price than he bought is a trader, but only he who buys that he may sell at a profit. If, on the contrary, he buys, not for sale, but for possession, and afterwards for some reason wishes to sell, it is not a trade transaction, even if he sell at a profit. For he may lawfully do this, either because he has bettered the thing, or because the value of the thing has changed with the change of place or time, or on account of the danger he incurs in transferring the thing from one place to another, or again in having it carried by hand. In this sense neither buying nor selling is unjust.' [1] The importance of this definition is that it rules out of the discussion all cases where the goods have been in any way improved or rendered more valuable by the services of the seller. Such improvement was always reckoned as the result of labour of one kind or another, and therefore entitled to remuneration. The essence of trade in the scholastic sense was selling the thing unchanged at a higher price than that at which it had been bought, for the sake of gain. [2]

The legitimacy of trade in this sense was only gradually admitted. The Fathers of the Church had with one voice condemned trade as being an occupation fraught with danger to the soul. Tertullian argued that there would be no need of trade if there were no desire for gain, and that there would be no desire for gain if man were not avaricious. Therefore avarice was the necessary basis of all trade.[3] St. Jerome thought that one man's gain in trading must always be another's loss ; and that, in any event, trade was a danger-ous occupation since it offered so many tempta-

---

[1] *Tractatus de Origine, etc., Monetarum,* ad. 2.

[2] ' Fit autem mercatio cum non ut emptor ea utatur sed ut eam carius vendat etiam non mutatam suo artificio ; illa mercatio dicitur proprie negotiatio ' (Biel, *op. cit.,* IV. XV. 10.)

[3] *De Idol.,* xi.

tions to fraud to the merchant.[1] St. Augustine proclaimed all trade evil because it turns men's minds away from seeking true rest, which is only to be found in God, and this opinion was embodied in the *Corpus Juris Canonici*.[2] This early view that all trade was to be indiscriminately condemned could not in the nature of things survive experience, and a great step forward was taken when Leo the Great pronounced that trade was neither good nor bad in itself, but was rendered good or bad according as it was honestly or dishonestly carried on.[3]

The scholastics, in addition to condemning commerce on the authority of the patristic texts, condemned it also on the Aristotelean ground that it was a chrematistic art, and this consideration, as we have seen above, enters into Aquinas's article on the subject.[4]

The extension of commercial life which took place about the beginning of the thirteenth century, raised acute controversies about the legitimacy of commerce. Probably nothing did more to broaden the teaching on this subject than the necessity of justifying trade which became more and more insistent after the Crusades.[5]

---

[1] Ashley, *op. cit.*, vol. i. pt. i. p. 129.
[2] See *Corpus Juris Canonici*, Decr. I. D. 88 c. 12.
[3] *Epist. ad Rusticum*, c. ix.   [4] Rambaud, *op. cit.*, p. 52.
[5] On the economic influence of the Crusades the following works may be consulted : Blanqui, *Histoire de l'Economie politique* ; Heeren, *Essai sur l'Influence politique et sociale des Croisades* ; Scherer, *Histoire du Commerce* ; Prutz, *Culturgeschichte der Kreuzzüge* ; Pigonneau, *Histoire du Commerce de la France* ; List, *Die Lehren der Handelspolitischen Geschichte*.

By the time of Aquinas the necessity of commerce had come to be fully realised, as appears from the passage in the *De Regimine Principum* : ' There are two ways in which it is possible to increase the affluence of any State. One, which is the more worthy way, is on account of the fertility of the country producing an abundance of all things which are necessary for human life, the other is through the employment of commerce, through which the necessaries of life are brought from different places. The former method can be clearly shown to be the more desirable. . . . It is more admirable that a State should possess an abundance of riches from its own soil than through commerce. For the State which needs a number of merchants to maintain its subsistence is liable to be injured in war through a shortage of food if communications are in any way impeded. Moreover, the influx of strangers corrupts the morals of many of the citizens . . . whereas, if the citizens themselves devote themselves to commerce, a door is opened to many vices. For when the desire of merchants is inclined greatly to gain, cupidity is aroused in the hearts of many citizens. . . . For the pursuit of a merchant is as contrary as possible to military exertion. For merchants abstain from labours, and while they enjoy the good things of life, they become soft in mind and their bodies are rendered weak and unsuitable for military exercises. . . . It therefore behoves the perfect State to make a moderate use of commerce.' [1]

[1] ii. 3.

Aquinas, who, as we have seen, recognised the necessity of commerce, did not condemn all trade indiscriminately, as the Fathers had done, but made the motive with which commerce was carried on the test of its legitimacy : ' Trade is justly deserving of blame, because, considered in itself, it satisfies the greed for gain, which knows no limit, and tends to infinity. Hence trading, considered in itself, has a certain debasement attaching thereto, in so far as, by its very nature, it does not imply a virtuous or necessary end. Nevertheless gain, which is the end of trading, though not implying, by its nature, anything virtuous or necessary, does not, in itself, connote anything sinful or contrary to virtue ; wherefore nothing prevents gain from being directed to some necessary or even virtuous end, and thus trading becomes lawful. Thus, for instance, a man may intend the moderate gain which he seeks to acquire by trading for the upkeep of his household, or for the assistance of the needy ; or again, a man may take to trade for some public advantage—for instance, lest his country lack the necessaries of life—and seek gain, not as an end, but as payment for his labour.' [1] This is important in connection with what we have said above as to property, as it shows that the trader was quite justified in seeking to obtain more profits, provided that they accrued for the benefit of the community. This justification of trade according to the end for which it was carried on, was not laid down for the first time by Aquinas, but may be found stated

[1] II. ii. 77, 4.

in an English treatise of the tenth century entitled *The Colloquy of Archbishop Alfric*, where, when a doctor asks a merchant if he wishes to sell his goods for the same price for which he has bought them, the merchant replies: 'I do not wish to do so, because if I do so, how would I be recompensed for my trouble? but I wish to sell them for more than I paid for them so that I might secure some gain wherewith to support myself, my wife, and family.' [1]

In spite of the fact that the earlier theory that no commercial gain which did not represent payment for labour could be justified was still maintained by some writers—for instance, Raymond de Pennafort [2]—the teaching of St. Thomas Aquinas was generally accepted throughout the later Middle Ages. Canonists and theologians accepted without hesitation the justification of trade formulated by Aquinas. [3] Henri de Gand, [4] Duns Scotus, [5] and François de Mayronis [6] unhesitatingly accepted the view of Aquinas, and incorporated it in their works. [7] ' An honourable merchant,' says Trithemius, ' who does not only think of large profits, and who is guided in all his dealings by the laws of God and man, and who gladly gives to the needy of his wealth and earnings, deserves the same esteem as any other worker. But it is no easy matter to be always honourable in all mer-

---

[1] Loria, *Analysi de la proprietà capitalista*, ii. 168.
[2] *Summa Theologica*, ii. vii. 5.
[3] Ashley, *op. cit.*, p. 55.   [4] *Quodlib.*, i. 40.
[5] *Lib. Quat. Sent.*, xv. 2.   [6] iv. 16, 4.
[7] See Jourdain, *op. cit.*, p. 20 *et seq.*

cantile dealings and not to become usurious. Without commerce no community can of course exist, but immoderate commerce is rather hurtful than beneficial, because it fosters greed of gain and gold, and enervates and emasculates the nation through love of pleasure and luxury.' [1] Nider says that to buy not for use but for sale at a higher price is called trade. Two special rules apply to this : first, that it should be useful to the State, and second, that the price should correspond to the diligence, prudence, and risk undertaken in the transaction.[2]

The later writers in the fifteenth century seem to have regarded trade more liberally even than Aquinas, although they quote his dictum on the subject as the basis of their teaching. Instead of condemning all commerce as wrong unless it was justified by good motives, they were rather inclined to treat commerce as being in itself colourless, but capable of becoming evil by bad motives. Carletus says : ' Commerce in itself is neither bad nor illegal, but it may become bad on account of the circumstances and the motive with which it is undertaken, the persons who undertake it, or the manner in which it is conducted. For instance, commerce undertaken through avarice or a desire for sloth is bad ; so also is commerce which is injurious to the republic, such as engrossing.' [3]

---

[1] Quoted in Janssen, *op. cit.*, vol. ii. p. 97.

[2] *Op. cit.*, iv. 10.

[3] *Summa Angelica*, 169 : ' Mercatio non est mala ex genere, sed bona, humano convictui necessaria dum fuerit justa. Mercatio simpliciter non est peccatum sed ejus abusus.' Biel, *op. cit.*, IV. xv. 10.

Endemann, having thoroughly studied all the fifteenth-century writers on the subject, says that commerce might be rendered unjustifiable either by subjective or objective reasons. Subjective illegality would arise from the person trading—for instance, the clergy—or the motive with which trade was undertaken; objective illegality on account of the object traded in, such as weapons in war-time, or the bodies of free men.[1] Speculative trading, and what we to-day call profiteering, were forbidden in all circumstances.[2]

We need not dwell upon the prohibition of trading by the clergy, because it was simply a rule of discipline which has not any bearing upon general economic teaching, except in so far as it shows that commerce was considered an occupation dangerous to virtue. Aquinas puts it as follows : ' Clerics should abstain not only from things that are evil in themselves, but even from those that have an appearance of evil. This happens in trading, both because it is directed to worldly gain, which clerics should despise, and because trading is open to so many vices, since "a merchant is hardly free from sins of the lips." ' [3] There is also another reason, because trading engages the mind too much with worldly cares, and consequently withdraws it from spiritual cares ; wherefore the Apostle says : [4] " No man

---

[1] *Studien*, vol. ii. p. 18.
[2] *The Ayenbite of Inwit*, a thirteenth-century confessor's manual, lays it down that speculation is a kind of usury. (Rambaud, *Histoire*, p. 56.)
[3] Eccles. xxvi. 28.   [4] 2 Tim. ii. 4.

being a soldier to God entangleth himself with
secular business." Nevertheless it is lawful for
clerics to engage in the first-mentioned kind of
exchange, which is directed to supply the necessaries of life, either by buying or by selling.' [1]
The rule of St. Benedict contains a strong ad-
monition to those who may be entrusted with the
sale of any of the products of the monastery, to
avoid all fraud and avarice.[2]

On the whole, the attitude towards commerce
seems to have grown more liberal in the course of
the Middle Ages. At first all commerce was condemned as sinful ; at a later period it was said to
be justifiable provided it was influenced by good
motives; while at a still later date the method of
treatment was rather to regard it as a colourless
act in itself which might be rendered harmful
by the presence of bad motives. This gradual
broadening of the justification of commerce is
probably a reflection of the necessities of the age,
which witnessed a very great expansion of commerce, especially of foreign trade. In the earlier
centuries remuneration for undertaking risk was
prohibited on the authority of a passage in the
Gregorian Decretals, but the later writers refused
to disallow it.[3] The following passage from Dr.
Cunningham's *Growth of English Industry and
Commerce* correctly represents the attitude of the
Church towards commerce at the end of the
Middle Ages : ' The ecclesiastic who regarded the

---

[1] *Summa*, II. ii. 77, 4, ad. 3.   [2] *Reg. St. Ben.*, 57.
[3] Cunningham, *Growth of English Industry and Commerce*, vol. i.
p. 255.

merchant as exposed to temptations in all his
dealings would not condemn him as sinful unless
it were clear that a transaction were entered on
solely for greed, and hence it was the tendency for
moralists to draw additional distinctions, and
refuse to pronounce against business practices
where common sense did not give the benefit of
the doubt.' [1] We have seen that one motive
which would justify the carrying on of trade was
the desire to support one's self and one's family.
Of course this motive was capable of bearing
a very extended and elastic interpretation, and
would justify increased commercial profits according as the standard of life improved. The other
motive given by the theologians, namely, the benefit of the State, was also one which was capable
of a very wide construction. One must remember
that even the manual labourer was bound not to
labour solely for avaricious gain, but also for the
benefit of his fellow-men. 'It is not only to
chastise our bodies,' says Basil, ' it is also by the
love of our neighbour that the labourer's life is
useful so that God may furnish through us our
weaker brethren ' ; [2] and a fifteenth-century book
on morality says : ' Man should labour for the
honour of God. He should labour in order to
gain for himself and his family the necessaries of
life and what will contribute to Christian joy,
and moreover to assist the poor and the sick by
his labours. He who acting otherwise seeks only
the pecuniary recompense of his work does ill,
and his labours are but usury. In the words of

---

[1] P. 255.   [2] *Reg. Fus. Tract.*, xxxvii. i.

St. Augustine, "thou shalt not commit usury with the work of thy hands, for thus wilt thou lose thy soul."'[1] The necessity for altruism and regard for the needs of one's neighbour as well as of one's self were therefore motives necessary to justify labour as well as commerce ; and it would be wrong to conclude that the teaching of the scholastics on the necessity for a good motive to justify trade operated to damp individual enterprise, or to discourage those who were inclined to launch commercial undertakings, any more than the insistence on the need for a similar motive in labourers was productive of idleness. What the mediæval teaching on commerce really amounted to was that, while commerce was as legitimate as any other occupation, owing to the numerous temptations to avarice and dishonesty which it involved, it must be carefully scrutinised and kept within due bounds. It was more difficult to insure the observance of the just price in the case of a sale by a merchant than in one by an artificer ; and the power which the merchant possessed of raising the price of the necessaries of life on the poor by engrossing and speculation rendered him a person whose operations should be carefully controlled.

Finally, it must be clearly understood that the attempt of some modern writers to base the mediæval justification of commerce on an analysis of all commercial gains as the payment for labour rests on a profound misunderstanding. As we have already pointed out, Aquinas distinctly

[1] Quoted in Janssen, *op. cit.*, vol. ii. p. 9.

rules out of consideration in his treatment of
commerce the case where the goods have been
improved in value by the exertions of the merchant.   When the element of labour entered into
the transaction the matter was clearly beyond
doubt, and the lengthy discussion devoted to the
question of commerce by Aquinas and his followers
shows that in justifying commercial gains they
were justifying a gain resting not on the remuneration for the labour, but on an independent title.

§ 8. *Cambium*

There was one department of commerce, namely,
cambium, or money-changing, which, while it did
not give any difficulty in theory, involved certain
difficulties in practice, owing to the fact that
it was liable to be used to disguise usurious
transactions.   Although *cambium* was, strictly
speaking, a special branch of commerce, it was
nevertheless usually treated in the works on usury,
the reason being that many apparent contracts of
cambium were in fact veiled loans, and that it was
therefore a matter of importance in discussing usury
to explain the tests by which genuine and usurious
exchanges could be distinguished.   Endemann
treats this subject very fully and ably ; [1] but for
the purpose of the present essay it is not necessary
to do more than to state the main conclusions at
which he arrives.
    Although the practice of exchange grew up
slowly and gradually during the later Middle

[1] *Studien*, vol. i. p. 75.

Ages, and, consequently, the amount of space
devoted to the discussion of the theory of exchange became larger as time went on, nevertheless there is no serious difference of opinion
between the writers of the thirteenth century, who
treat the subject in a fragmentary way, and those
of the fifteenth, who deal with it exhaustively
and systematically. Aquinas does not mention
cambium in the *Summa,* but he recognises the
necessity for some system of exchange in the *De
Regimine Principum.*[1] All the later writers who
mention *cambium* are agreed in regarding it as a
species of commerce to which the ordinary rules
regulating all commerce apply. Francis de Mayronis says that the art of *cambium* is as natural
as any other kind of commerce, because of the
diversity of the currencies in different kingdoms,
and approves of the campsor receiving some
remuneration for his labour and trouble.[2] Nicholas
de Ausmo, in his commentary on the *Summa
Pisana,* written in the beginning of the fifteenth
century, says that the campsor may receive a gain
from his transactions, provided that they are not
conducted with the sole object of making a profit,
and that the gain he may receive must be limited
by the common estimation of the place and time.
This is practically saying that *cambium* may be
carried on under the same conditions as any other
species of commerce. Biel says that *cambium*

---

[1] ' Cum enim extraneae monetae communicantur in permutationibus
oportet recurrere ad artem campsoriam, cum talia numismata non
tantum valeant in regionibus extraneis quantum in propriis (*De Reg.
Prin.,* ii. 13). [2] In *Quot. Lib. Sent.,* iv. 16, 4.

is only legitimate if the campsor has the motive
of keeping up a family or benefiting the State,
and that the contract may become usurious if the
gain is not fair and moderate.[1] The right of the
campsor to some remuneration for risk was only
gradually admitted, and forms the subject of much
discussion amongst the jurists.[2] This hesitation
in allowing remuneration for risk was not peculiar
to *cambium*, but, as we have seen above, was
common to all commerce. Endemann points out
how the theologians and jurists unanimously insisted that *cambium* could not be justified except
when the just price was observed, and that, when
the doctrine attained its full development, the
element of labour was but one of the constituents
in the estimation of that price.[3]

All the writers who treated of exchange divided
it into three kinds ; ordinary exchange of the
moneys of different currencies (*cambium minutum*),
exchange of moneys of different currencies between
different places, the justification for which rested
on remuneration for an imaginary transport
(*cambium per litteras*), and usurious exchange of
moneys of the same currency (*cambium siccum*).
The former two species of cambium were justifiable, whereas the last was condemned.[4]

The most complete treatise on the subject of
money exchange is that of Thomas da Vio, written
in 1499. The author of this treatise divides money-

[1] *Op. cit.*, IV. xv. 11.
[2] Endemann, *Studien*, vol. i. pp. 123-36.
[3] *Ibid.*, p. 213.
[4] Laurentius de Rodulfis, *De Usuris*, pt. iii. Nos. 1 to 5.

changing into three kinds, just, unjust, and doubtful.   There were three kinds of just change ; *cambium minutum*, in which the campsor was entitled
to a reasonable remuneration for his labour;
cambium per litteras, in which the campsor was
held entitled to a wage (*merces*) for an imaginary
transportation ; and thirdly, when the campsor
carried money from one place to another, where it
was of higher value.   The unjust change was
when the contract was a usurious transaction veiled
in the guise of a genuine exchange.   Under the
doubtful changes, the author discusses various
special points which need not detain us here.

Thomas da Vio then goes on to discuss whether
the justifiable exchange can be said to be a species
of loan, and concludes that it can not, because all
that the campsor receives is an indemnity against
loss and a remuneration for his labour, trouble,
outlay, and risk, which is always justifiable.   He
then goes on to state the very important principle,
that in *cambium* money is not to be considered
a measure of value, but a vendible commodity,[1]
a distinction which Endemann thinks was productive of very important results in the later
teaching on the subject.[2]   The last question
treated in the treatise is the measure of the
campsor's profit, and here the contract of exchange
is shown to be on all fours with every other contract, because the essential principle laid down

---

[1] 'Numisma quamvis sit mensura et instrumentum in permutationibus ; tamen per se aliquid esse potest.' It is this principle that
justifies the treatment of *cambium* in this section rather than the next.

[2] *Studien*, vol. ii. p. 212.

for determining its justice is the observance of the equivalence between both parties.[1]

SECTION 2.—THE SALE OF THE USE OF MONEY

§ 1. *Usury in Greece and Rome*

The prohibition of usury has always occupied such a large place in histories of the Middle Ages, and particularly in discussions relating to the attitude of the Church towards economic questions, that it is important that its precise foundation and extent should be carefully studied. The usury prohibition has been the centre of so many bitter controversies, that it has almost become part of the stock-in-trade of the theological mob orators. The attitude of the Church towards usury only takes a slightly less prominent place than its attitude towards Galileo in the utterances of those who are anxious to convict it of error. We have referred to this current controversy, not in order that we might take a part in it, but that, on the contrary, we might avoid it. It is no part of our purpose in our treatment of this subject to discuss whether the usury prohibition was or was not suitable to the conditions of the Middle Ages; whether it did or did not impede industrial enterprise and commercial expansion; or whether it was or was not universally disregarded and evaded in real life. These are inquiries which, though full of interest, would not

---

[1] Brants has a very luminous and interesting section on *Cambium*, *op. cit.*, p. 214 *et seq.*

be in place in a discussion of theory. All we are concerned to do in the following pages is to indicate the grounds on which the prohibition of usury rested, the precise extent of its application, and the conceptions of economic theory which it indicated and involved.

We must remark in the first place that the prohibition of usury was in no sense peculiar to the Catholic Church in the Middle Ages, but, on the contrary, was to be found in many other religious and legal systems—for instance, in the writings of the Greek and Roman philosophers, amongst the Jews, and the followers of Mohammed. We shall give a very brief account of the other prohibitions of usury before coming to deal with the scholastic teaching on the subject.

We can find no trace of any legal prohibition of usury in ancient Greece. Although Solon's laws contained many provisions for the relief of poor debtors, they did not forbid the taking of interest, nor did they limit the rate of interest that might be taken.[1] In Rome the Twelve Tables fixed a maximum rate of interest, which was probably ten or twelve per cent. per annum, but which cannot be determined with certainty owing to the doubtful signification of the expression ' *unciarum foenus.*' The legal rate of interest was gradually reduced until the year 347 B.C., when five per cent. was fixed as a maximum. In 342 B.C. interest was forbidden altogether by the Genucian Law ; but this law, though never repealed, was in practice quite inoperative owing to the facility with

[1] Cleary, *The Church and Usury*, p. 21.

which it could be evaded; and consequently the
oppression of borrowers was prevented by the
enactment, or perhaps it would be more correct to
say the general recognition, of a maximum rate
of interest of twelve per cent. per annum. This
maximum rate—the *Centesima*—remained in operation until the time of Justinian.[1] Justinian,
who was under the influence of Christian teaching,
and who might therefore be expected to have
regarded usury with unfavourable eyes, fixed the
following maximum rates of interest—maritime
loans twelve per cent. ; loans to ordinary persons,
not in business, six per cent. ; loans to high per-
sonages (*illustres*) and agriculturists, four per cent.[2]

While the taking of interest was thus approved
or tolerated by Greek and Roman law, it was at
the same time reprobated by the philosophers of
both countries. Plato objects to usury because
it tends to set one class, the poor or the borrowers,
against another, the rich or the lenders ; and goes
so far as to make it wrong for the borrower to
repay either the principal or interest of his debt.
He further considers that the profession of the
usurer is to be despised, as it is an illiberal and
debasing way of making money.[3] While Plato
therefore disapproves in no ambiguous words of
usury, he does not develop the philosophical bases
of his objection, but is content to condemn it
rather for its probable ill effects than on account
of its inherent injustice.

---

[1] Hunter, *Roman Law*, pp. 652-53 ; Cleary, *op. cit.*, pp. 22-6 ;
Roscher, *Political Economy*, s. 90.

[2] *Code* 4, 32, 26, 1.   [3] *Laws*, v. ch. 11-13.

Aristotle condemns usury because it is the most extreme and dangerous form of chrematistic acquisition, or the art of making money for its own sake. As we have seen above, in discussing the legitimacy of commerce, buying cheap and selling dear was one form of chrematistic acquisition, which could only be justified by the presence of certain motives; and usury, according to the philosopher, was a still more striking example of the same kind of acquisition, because it consisted in making money from money, which was thus employed for a function different from that for which it had been originally invented. 'Usury is most reasonably detested, as the increase of our fortune arises from the money itself, and not by employing it for the purpose for which it was intended. For it was devised for the sake of exchange, but usury multiplies it. And hence usury has received the name of τόκος, or produce; for whatever is produced is itself like its parents; and usury is merely money born of money; so that of all means of money-making it is the most contrary to nature.'[1] We need not pause here to discuss the precise significance of Aristotle's conceptions on this subject, as they are to us not so much of importance in themselves, as because they suggested a basis for the treatment of usury to Aquinas and his followers.[2]

In Rome, as in Greece, the philosophers and moralists were unanimous in their condemnation of the practice of usury. Cicero condemns usury as being hateful to mankind, and makes Cato say

[1] Aristotle, *Politics*, i. 10.   [2] Cleary, *op. cit.*, p. 29.

that it is on the same level of moral obliquity as
murder ; and Seneca makes a point that became
of some importance in the Middle Ages, namely,
that usury is wrongful because it involves the
selling of time.[1] Plutarch develops the argument
that money is sterile, and condemns the practices of contemporary money-lenders as unjust.[2]
The teaching of the philosophers as to the unlaw-
fulness of usury was reflected in the popular feeling of the time.[3]

§ 2. Usury in the Old Testament

The question of usury therefore attracted considerable attention in the teaching and practice
of pagan antiquity. It occupied an equally important place in the Old Testament. In Exodus
we find the first prohibition of usury : ' If thou
lend money to any of my people being poor, thou
shalt not be to him as a creditor, neither shall ye
lay upon him usury.' [4] In Leviticus we read :
' And if thy brother be waxen poor, and his hand
fail with thee ; then thou must uphold him ; as
a stranger and a sojourner shall he live with thee.
Take thou no money of him or increase, but fear
thy God that thy brother may live with thee.
Thou shalt not give him thy money upon usury,
nor give him victuals for increase.' [5] Deuteronomy
lays down a wider prohibition : ' Thou shalt not
lend upon usury to thy brother ; usury of money,
usury of victuals, usury of anything that is lent

[1] Cleary, op. cit., p. 29.   [2] De Vitando Aere Alieno.
[3] Espinas, op. cit., pp. 81-2 ; Roscher, Political Economy, s. 90.
[4] Exod. xxii. 25.   [5] Lev. xxv. 35.

upon usury ; unto a foreigner thou mayest lend
upon usury, but unto thy brother thou mayest not
lend upon usury.' [1] It will be noticed that the
first and second of these texts do not forbid usury
except in the case of loans to the poor, and, if we
had them alone to consider, we could conclude
that loans to the rich or to business men were
allowed. The last text, however, extends the
prohibition to all loans to one's brother—an
expression which was of importance in Christian
times, as Christian writers maintained the universal brotherhood of man.

It is unnecessary for us to discuss the underlying considerations which prompted these
ordinances. Dr. Cleary, who has studied the
matter with great care, concludes that: 'The
legislator was urged mostly by economic considerations. . . . The permission to extract usury
from strangers—a permission which later writers,
such as Maimonides, regarded as a command—
clearly favours the view that the legislator was
guided by economic principles. It is more difficult to say whether he based his legislation on the
principle that usury is intrinsically unjust—that
is to say, unjust even when taken in moderation.
There is really nothing in the texts quoted to
enable us to decide. The universality of the
prohibition when there is question solely of Jews
goes to show that usury as such was regarded as
unjust ; whilst its permission as between Jew
and Gentile favours the contradictory hypothesis.' [2] Modern Jewish thought is inclined to

[1] Deut. xxiii. 19.   [2] *Op. cit.*, pp. 5-6.

hold the view that these prohibitions were based upon the assumption that usury was intrinsically unjust, but that the taking of usury from the Gentiles was justified on the principle of compensation; in other words, that Jews might exact usury from those who might exact it from them.[1] It is at least certain that usury was regarded by the writers of the Old Testament as amongst the most terrible of sins.[2]

The general attitude of the Jews towards usury cannot be better explained than by quoting Dr. Cleary's final conclusion on the subject: ' It appears therefore that in the Old Testament usury was universally prohibited between Israelite and Israelite, whilst it was permitted between Israelite and Gentile. Furthermore, it seems impossible to decide what was the nature of the obligations imposed—whether the prohibition supposed and ratified an already existing universal obligation, in charity or justice, or merely imposed a new obligation in obedience, binding the consciences of men for economic or political reasons. So, too, it seems impossible to decide absolutely whether the decrees were intended to possess eternal validity ; the probabilities, however, seem to favour very strongly the view that they were intended as mere economic regulations suited to the circumstances of the time. This does not, of course, decide the other question, whether, apart from such positive regulations,

[1] *Jewish Encyclopædia,* art. ' Usury.'
[2] Ezek. xviii. 13 ; Jer. xv. 10 ; Ps. xiv. 5, cix. 11, cxii. 5 ; Prov. xxviii. 8 ; Hes. xviii. 8 ; 2 Esd. v. 1 *et seq.*

there already existed an obligation arising from the natural law ; nor would the passing of the positive law into desuetude affect the existence of the other obligation.' [1]

Before we pass from the consideration of the Old Testament to that of the New, we may mention that the taking of interest by Mohammedans is forbidden in the Koran. [2]

§ 3. *Usury in the First Twelve Centuries of Christianity.*

The only passage in the Gospels which bears directly on the question of usury is a verse of St. Luke, the correct reading of which is a matter of considerable difference of opinion. [3] The Revised Version reads : ' But love your enemies, and do them good, and lend, never despairing (*nihil desperantes*) ; and your reward shall be great.' If this be the true reading of the verse, it does not touch the question of usury at all, as it is simply an exhortation to lend without worrying whether the debtor fail or not. [4] The more generally received reading of this verse, however, is that adopted by the Vulgate, ' mutuum date, nihil inde sperantes '—' lend hoping for nothing thereby.' If this be the correct reading, the verse raises considerable difficulties of interpretation. It may simply mean, as Mastrofini in-

---

[1] *Op. cit.*, pp. 17-18.

[2] ii. 30. This prohibition is universally evaded. (Roscher, *Political Economy*, s. 90.)   [3] Luke vi. 35.

[4] Cleary, *op. cit.*, p. 33, following Knabenbaur.

terprets it, that all human actions should be
performed, not in the hope of obtaining any
material reward, but for the love of God and our
neighbour ; or it may contain an actual precept
or counsel relating to the particular subject of
loans. If the latter be the correct interpretation,
the further question arises whether the recommendation is to renounce merely the interest of
a loan or the principal as well. We need not here
engage on the details of the controversy thus
aroused ; it is sufficient to say that it is the
almost unanimous opinion of modern authorities
that the verse recommends the renunciation of
the principal as well as the interest ; and that, if
this interpretation is correct, the recommendation
is not a precept, but a counsel.[1] Aquinas thought
that the verse was a counsel as to the repayment
of the principal, but a precept as to the payment
of interest, and this opinion is probably correct.[2]
With the exception of this verse, there is not a
single passage in the Gospels which prohibits the
taking of usury.

We must now give some account of the teaching
on usury which was laid down by the Fathers and
early councils of the Church ; but at the same
time we shall not attempt to treat this in an
exhaustive way, because, although the early
Christian teaching is of interest in itself, it exercised little or no influence upon the great philosophical treatment of the same subject by Aquinas
and his followers, which is the principal subject
to be discussed in these pages. The first thing we

[1] Cleary, op. cit., p. 34. [2] Ibid., p. 35.

must remark is that the prohibition of usury was
not included by the Council of Jerusalem amongst
the 'necessary things' imposed upon converts
from the Gentiles.[1] This would seem to show
that the taking of usury was not regarded as unlawful by the Apostles, who were at pains expressly to forbid the commission of offences, the
evil of which must have appeared plainly from
the natural law—for instance, fornication. The
Didache, which was used as a book of catechetical
instruction for catechumens, does not specifically
mention usury ; the forcing of the repayment
of loans from the poor who are unable to pay is
strongly reprobated ; but this is not so in the case
of the rich.[2] Clement of Alexandria expressly
limits his disapprobation of usury to the case of
loans between brothers, whom he defines as
'participators in the same word,' i.e. fellow-
Christians ; and in any event it is clear that he
regards it as sin against charity, but not against
justice.[3]

Tertullian is one of the first of the Fathers to
lay down positively that the taking of usury is
sinful. He regards it as obviously wrong for
Christians to exact usury on their loans, and
interprets the passage of St. Luke, to which we
have referred, as a precept against looking for
even the repayment of the principal.[4] On the
other hand, Cyprian, writing in the same century,
although he declaims eloquently and vigorously
against the usurious practices of the clergy, does

[1] Acts xv. 29.   [2] Didache, ch. i. ; Cleary, op. cit., p. 39.
[3] Stromata, ii. 18.   [4] Ad Marcion, iv. 17.

not specifically express the opinion that the taking of usury is wrong in itself.[1]

Thus, during the first three centuries of Christianity, there does not seem to have been, as far as we can now ascertain, any definite and general doctrine laid down on the subject of usury. In the year 305 or 306 a very important step forward was taken, when the Council of Elvira passed a decree against usury. This decree, as given by Ivo and Gratian, seems only to have applied to usury on the part of the clergy, but as given by Mansi it affected the clergy and laity alike. ' Should any cleric be found to have taken usury,' the latter version runs, ' let him be degraded and excommunicated. Moreover, if any layman shall be proved a usurer, and shall have promised, when corrected, to abstain from the practice, let him be pardoned. If, on the contrary, he perseveres in his evil-doing, he is to be excommunicated.' [2] Although the Council of Elvira was but a provincial Council, its decrees are important, as they provided a model for later legislation. Dr. Cleary thinks that Mansi's version of this decree is probably incorrect, and that, therefore, the Council only forbade usury on the part of the clergy. In any event, with this one possible and extremely doubtful exception, there was no conciliar legislation affecting the practice of usury on the part of the laity until the eighth century. Certain individual popes censured the taking of usury by laymen, and the Council of Nice expressed

[1] *Le Lapsis,* ch. 5-6 ; Cleary, *op. cit.,* pp. 42-3.
[2] Cleary, *op. cit.,* p. 43.

the opinion that such a practice was contrary to Christ's teaching, but there is nowhere to be found an imperative and definite prohibition of the taking of usury except by the clergy.[1]

The inconclusive result of the Christian teaching up to the middle of the fourth century is well summarised by Dr. Cleary : ' Hitherto we have encountered mere prohibitions of usury with little or no attempt to assign a reason for them other than that of positive legislation. Most of the statements of these early patristic writers, as well as possibly all of the early Christian legislative enactments, deal solely with the practice of usury by the clergy ; still, there is sufficient evidence to show that in those days it was reprobated even for the Christian laity, for the *Didache* and Tertullian clearly teach or presuppose its prohibition, while the oecumenical Council of Nice certainly presupposed its illegality for the laity, though it failed to sustain its doctrinal presuppositions with corresponding ecclesiastical penalties.   With the exception of some very vague statements by Cyprian and Clement of Alexandria, we find no attempt to state the nature of the resulting obligation—that is to say, we are not told whether there is an obligation of obedience, of justice, or of charity.   The prohibition indeed seems to be regarded as universal ; and it may very well be contended that for the cases the Fathers consider it was in fact universal—for the loans with which they are concerned, being necessitous, should be, in accordance with Christian

[1] Cleary, *op. cit.*, pp. 44-8.

charity, gratuitous—even if speculatively usurious loans in general were not unjust.' [1]

The middle of the fourth century marked the opening of a new period—' a period when oratorical denunciations are profuse, and when consequently philosophical speculation, though fairly active, is of too imaginative a character to be sufficiently definite.' [2] St. Basil's *Homilies on the Fourteenth Psalm* contain a violent denunciation of usury, the reasoning of which was repeated by St. Gregory of Nyssa [3] and St. Ambrose.[4] These three Fathers draw a terrible picture of the state of the poor debtor, who, harassed by his creditors, falls deeper and deeper into despair, until he finally commits suicide, or has to sell his children into slavery. Usury was therefore condemned by these Fathers as a sin against charity ; the passage from St. Luke was looked on merely as a counsel in so far as it related to the repayment of the principal, but as a precept so far as it related to usury ; but the notion that usury was in its very essence a sin against justice does not appear to have arisen. The natural sterility of money is referred to, but not developed ; and it is suggested, though not categorically stated, that usury may be taken from wealthy debtors.[5]

The other Fathers of the later period do not throw very much light on the question of how usury was regarded by the early Church. St. Hilary [6] and Jerome [7] still base their objection

---

[1] *Op. cit.*, pp. 48-9.   [2] Cleary, *op. cit.*, p. 49.
[3] *Contra Usurarios.*   [4] *De Tobia.*   [5] Cleary, *op. cit.*, p. 52.
[6] In Ps. xiv.   [7] *Ad Ezech.*

on the ground of its being an offence against
charity ; and St. Augustine, though he would like
to make restitution of usury a duty, treats the
matter from the same point of view.[1] On the
other hand, there are to be found patristic utterances in favour of the legality of usury, and
episcopal approbations of civil codes which permitted it.[2] The civil law did not attempt to
suppress usury, but simply to keep it within due
bounds.[3] The result of the patristic teaching
therefore was on the whole unsatisfactory and
inconclusive. ' Whilst patristic opinion,' says Dr.
Cleary, ' is very pronounced in condemning usury,
the condemnation is launched against it more
because of its oppressiveness than for its intrinsic
injustice. As Dr. Funk has pointed out, one
can scarcely cite a single patristic opinion which
can be said clearly to hold that usury is against
justice, whilst there are, on the contrary, certain
undercurrents of thought in many writers, and
certain explicit statements in others, which tend
to show that the Fathers would not have been prepared to deal so harshly with usurers, did usurers
not treat their debtors so cruelly. . . . Of keen
philosophical analysis there is none. . . . On the
whole, we find the teachings of the Fathers crude
and undeveloped.' [4]

The practical teaching with regard to the taking

---

[1] Cleary, op. cit., p. 56.   [2] Ibid., pp. 56-7.
[3] Justinian Code, iv. 32.
[4] Op. cit., pp. 57-9. On the patristic teaching on usury, see Espinas,
op. cit., pp. 82-4 ; Roscher, Political Economy, s. 90 ; Antoine, Cours
d'Economie sociale, pp. 588 et seq.

of usury made an important advance in the eighth
and ninth centuries, although the philosophical
analysis of the subject did not develop any more
fully. A capitulary canon made in 789 decreed
' that each and all are forbidden to give anything
on usury ' ; and a capitulary of 813 states that
' not only should the Christian clergy not demand
usury, laymen should not.'   In 825 it was decreed that the counts were to assist the bishops in
their suppression of usury ; and in 850 the Synod
of Ticinum bound usurers to restitution.[1] The
underlying principles of these enactments is as
obscure as their meaning is plain and definite.
There is not a single trace of the keen analysis
with which Aquinas was later to illuminate and
adorn the subject.

§ 4. *The Mediæval Prohibition of Usury*

The tenth and eleventh centuries saw no
advance in the teaching on usury. The twelfth
century, however, ushered in a new era. ' Before
that century controversy had been mostly confined to theologians, and treated theologically,
with reference to God and the Bible, and only
rarely with regard to economic considerations.
After the twelfth century the discussion was
conducted on a gradually broadening economic
basis—appeals to the Fathers, canonists, philosophers, the *jus divinum*, the *jus naturale*, the

[1] These are but a few of the enactments of the period directed
against usury (Cleary, *op. cit.*, p. 61 ; Favre, *Le prêt à intérêt dans
l'ancienne France*).

jus humanum, became the order of the day.' [1]
Before we proceed to discuss the new philosophical
or scholastic treatment of usury which was in-
augurated for all practical purposes by Aquinas,
we must briefly refer to the ecclesiastical legislation on the subject.

In 1139 the second Lateran Council issued a
very strong declaration against usurers. ' We
condemn that disgraceful and detestable rapacity,
condemned alike by human and divine law, by
the Old and the New Testaments, that insati-
able rapacity of usurers, whom we hereby cut off
from all ecclesiastical consolation ; and we order
that no archbishop, bishop, abbot, or cleric shall
receive back usurers except with the very greatest
caution, but that, on the contrary, usurers are to
be regarded as infamous, and shall, if they do not
repent, be deprived of Christian burial.' [2]   It
might be argued that this decree was aimed against
immoderate or habitual usury, and not against
usury in general, but all doubt as regards the
attitude of the Church was set at rest by a decree
of the Lateran Council of 1179.   This decree runs :
' Since almost in every place the crime of usury
has become so prevalent that many people give
up all other business and become usurers, as if it
were lawful, regarding not its prohibition in both
Testaments, we ordain that manifest usurers shall
not be admitted to communion, nor, if they die
in their sins, be admitted to Christian burial, and
that no priest shall accept their alms.' [3]   Mean-

---

[1] Bohm-Bawerk, *Capital and Interest*, p. 19.
[2] Cleary, *op. cit.*, p. 64.   [3] *Ibid.*

while, Alexander III., having given much attention to the subject of usury, had come to the conclusion that it was a sin against justice. This recognition of the essential injustice of usury marked a turning-point in the history of the treatment of the subject; and Alexander III. seems entitled to be designated the 'pioneer of its scientific study.'[1] Innocent III. followed Alexander in the opinion that usury was unjust in itself, and from his time forward there was but little further disagreement upon the matter amongst the theologians.[2]

In 1274 Gregory X., in the Council of Lyons, ordained that no community, corporation, or individual should permit foreign usurers to hire houses, but that they should expel them from their territory; and the disobedient, if prelates, were to have their lands put under interdict, and, if laymen, to be visited by their ordinary with ecclesiastical censures.[3] By a further canon he ordained that the wills of usurers who did not make restitution should be invalid.[4] This brought usury definitely within the jurisdiction of the ecclesiastical courts.[5] In 1311 the Council of Vienne declared all secular legislation in favour of usury null and void, and branded as heresy the belief that usury was not sinful.[6] The precise extent and interpretation of this decree have given rise to a considerable amount of discussion,[7]

---

[1] Cleary, op. cit., p. 65.
[2] Ibid., p. 68.
[3] Liber Sextus, v. 5, 1.
[4] Ibid., c. 2.
[5] Ashley, op. cit., vol. i. pt. i. p. 150.
[6] Clementinarum, v. 5, 1.
[7] Cleary, op. cit., pp. 74-8.

which need not detain us here, because by that
time the whole question of usury had come under
the treatment of the great scholastic writers,
whose teaching is more particularly the subject
matter of the present essay.

Even as late as the first half of the thirteenth
century there was no serious discussion of usury
by the theologians. William of Paris, Alexander
of Hales, and Albertus Magnus simply pronounced
it sinful on account of the texts in the Old and
New Testaments, which we have quoted above.[1]
It was Aquinas who really put the teaching on
usury upon the new foundation, which was destined to support it for so many hundred years,
and which even at the present day appeals to
many sympathetic and impartial inquirers. Mr.
Lecky apologises for the obscurity of his account
of the argument of Aquinas, but adds that the
confusion is chiefly the fault of the latter ; [2] but
the fact that Mr. Lecky failed to grasp the meaning
of the argument should not lead one to conclude
that the argument itself was either confused or
illogical. The fact that it for centuries remained
the basis of the Catholic teaching on the subject
is a sufficient proof that its inherent absurdity
did not appear apparent to many students at least
as gifted as Mr. Lecky. We shall quote the article
of Aquinas at some length, because it was universally accepted by all the theologians of the
fourteenth and fifteenth centuries, with whose
opinions we are concerned in this essay. To

[1] Jourdain, *op. cit.*, p. 15.
[2] *Rise and Influence of Rationalism in Europe*, vol. ii. p. 261.

quote later writings is simply to repeat in different words the conclusions at which Aquinas arrived.[1]

In answer to the question ' whether it is a sin to take usury for money lent,' Aquinas replies : ' To take usury for money lent is unjust in itself, because this is to sell what does not exist, and this evidently leads to inequality, which is contrary to justice.

' In order to make this evident, we must observe that there are certain things the use of which consists in their consumption ; thus we consume wine when we use it for drink, and we consume wheat when we use it for food. Wherefore in such-like things the use of the thing must not be reckoned apart from the thing itself, and whoever is granted the use of the thing is granted the thing itself ; and for this reason to lend things of this kind is to transfer the ownership. Accordingly, if a man wanted to sell wine separately from the use of the wine, he would be selling the same thing twice, or he would be selling what does not exist, wherefore he would evidently commit a sin of injustice. In like manner he commits an injustice who lends wine or wheat, and asks for double payment, viz. one, the return of the thing in equal measure, the other, the price of the use, which is called usury.

' On the other hand, there are other things the use of which does not consist in their consumption ; thus to use a house is to dwell in it, not to destroy it. Wherefore in such things both may be granted ; for instance, one man may hand over

[1] Endemann, *Studien*, vol. i. p. 17.

to another the ownership of his house, while reserving to himself the use of it for a time, or, *vice versa*, he may grant the use of a house while retaining the ownership. For this reason a man may lawfully make a charge for the use of his house, and, besides this, revendicate the house from the person to whom he has granted its use, as happens in renting and letting a house.

'But money, according to the philosopher,[1] was invented chiefly for the purpose of exchange ; and consequently the proper and principal use of money is its consumption or alienation, whereby it is sunk in exchange. Hence it is by its very nature unlawful to take payment for the use of money lent, which payment is known as usury ; and, just as a man is bound to restore other ill-gotten goods, so he is bound to restore the money which he has taken in usury.'[2]

The essential thing to notice in this explanation is that the contract of *muiuum* is shown to be a sale. The distinction between things which are consumed in use (*res fungibiles*), and which are not consumed in use (*res non fungibiles*) was familiar to the civil lawyers ; but what they had never perceived was precisely what Aquinas perceived, namely, that the loan of a fungible thing was in fact not a loan at all, but a sale, for the simple reason that the ownership in the thing passed. Once the transaction had been shown to be a sale, the principle of justice to be applied to it became obvious. As we have seen above, in treating of sales, the essential basis of justice in exchange was

[1] *Eth.*, v. *Pol.* 1.   [2] II. ii. 78, 1.

the observance of *aequalitas* between buyer and seller—in other words, the fixing of a just price. The contract of *mutuum*, however, was nothing else than a sale of fungibles, and therefore the just price in such a contract was the return of fungibles of the same value as those lent. If the particular fungible sold happened to be money, the estimation of the just price was a simple matter—it was the return of an amount of money of equal value. As money happened to be the universal measure of value, this simply meant the return of the same amount of money. Those who maintained that something additional might be claimed for the use of the money lost sight of the fact that the money was incapable of being used apart from its being consumed.[1] To ask for payment for the sale of a thing which not only did not exist, but which was quite incapable of existence, was clearly to ask for something for nothing—which obviously offended against the first principles of commutative justice. ' He that is not bound to lend,' says Aquinas in another part of the same article, ' may accept repayment for what he has done, but he must not exact more. Now he is repaid according to equality of justice

---

[1] Aquinas did not lose sight of the fact that money might, in certain cases, be used apart from being consumed—for instance, when it was not used as a means of exchange, but as an ornament. He gives the example of money being sewn up and sealed in a bag to prevent its being spent, and in this condition lent for any purpose. In this case, of course, the transaction would not be a *mutuum*, but a *locatio et conductio*, and therefore a price could be charged for the use of the money (*Quaestiones Disputatae de Malo*, Q. xiii. art. iv. ad. 15, quoted in Cronin's *Ethics*, vol. ii. p. 332).

if he is repaid as much as he lent, wherefore, if he exacts more for the usufruct of a thing which has no other use but the consumption of its substance, he exacts a price of something non-existent, and so his exaction is unjust.' [1] And in the next article the principle that *mutuum* is a sale appears equally clearly : ' Money cannot be sold for a greater sum than the amount lent, which has to be paid back.' [2]

The difficulty which moderns find in understanding this teaching, is that it is said to be based on the sterility of money. A moment's thought, however, will convince us that money is in fact sterile until labour has been applied to it. In this sense money differs in its essence from a cow or a tree. A cow will produce calves, or a tree will produce fruit without the application of any exertion by its owner ; but, whatever profit is derived from money, is derived from the use to which it is put by the person who owns it. This is all that the scholastics meant by the sterility of money. They never thought of denying that money, when properly used, was capable of bringing its employer a profit ; but they emphatically

[1] II. ii. 78, 1, ad. 5.
[2] II. ii. 78, 2, ad. 4.   Biel distinguishes three kinds of exchange: of goods for goods, or barter ; of goods for money, or sale ; and of money for money ; and adds, ' In his contractibus . . . generaliter justitia in hoc consistit quod fiant sine fraude, et servetur aequalitas substantiae, qualitatis, quantitatis in commutatis (*op. cit.*, IV. xv. 1). Buridan says that usury is contrary to natural law ' ex conditione justitiae quae in aequalitate damni et lucri consistit; quoniam injustum est pro re semel commutata pluries pretium recipere ' (In *Lib. Pol.*, iv. 6).

asserted that the profit was due to the labour, and not to the money.

Antoninus of Florence clearly realised this: ' Money is not profitable of itself alone, nor can it multiply itself, but it may become profitable through its employment by merchants ' ; [1] and Bernardine of Sienna says : ' Money has not simply the character of money, but it has beyond this a productive character, which we commonly call capital.' [2] ' What is money,' says Brants, ' if it is not a means of exchange, of which the employment and preservation will give a profit, if he who possesses it is prudent, active, and intelligent ? If this money is well employed, it will become a capital, and one may derive a profit from it ; but this profit arises from the activity of him who uses it, and consequently this profit belongs to him—it is the fruit, the remuneration of his labour. . . . Did they (the scholastics) say that it was impossible to draw a profit from a sum of money ? No ; they admitted fully that one might *de pecunia lucrari* ; but this *lucrum* does not come from the *pecunia,* but from the application of labour to the sum.' [3]

Therefore, if the borrower did not derive any profit from the loan, the sum lent had in fact been sterile, and obviously the just price of the loan was the return of the amount lent ; if, on the contrary, the borrower had made a profit from it, it was the reward of his labour, and not the fruit of the loan itself. To repay more than the sum

---

[1] Quoted in Brants, *op. cit.,* p. 134.   [2] *Ibid.*
[3] Brants, *op. cit.,* pp. 133-5 ; Nider, *De Cont. Merc.* iii. 15.

lent would therefore be to make a payment to
one person for the labour of another.[1] The exaction of usury was therefore the exploitation of
another man's exertion.[2]

It is interesting to notice how closely the rules
applying in the case of sales were applied to usury.
The raising of the price of a loan on account of
some special benefit derived from it by the borrower
is precisely analogous to raising the sale price of
an object because it is of some special individual
utility to the buyer. On the other hand, as we
shall see further down, any special damage
suffered by the lender was a sufficient reason for
exacting something over and above the amount
lent ; this was precisely the rule that applied in
the case of sales, when the seller suffered any
special damage from parting with the object sold.
Thus the analogy between sales and loans was
complete at every point. In both, equality of
sacrifice was the test of justice.

Nor could it be suggested that the delay in the
repayment of the loan was a reason for increasing the amount to be repaid, because this really
amounted to a sale of time, which, of its nature,
could not be owned.[3]

---

[1] Gerson, *De Cont.*, iv. 15.

[2] Neumann, when he says that ' it was sinful to recompense the use
of capital belonging to another ' (*Geschichte des Wuchers in Deutschland,*
p. 25), seems to miss the whole point of the discussion. The teaching
of the canonists on rents and partnership shows clearly that the
owner of capital might draw a profit from another's labour, and the
central point of the usury teaching was that money which has been
lent, and employed so as to produce a profit by the borrower, belongs
not ' to another,' but to the very man who employed it, namely, the
borrower.   [3] Rambaud, *op. cit.*, p. 63 ; Aquinas (?), *De Usuris*, i. 4.

The scholastic teaching, then, on the subject was quite plain and unambiguous. Usury, or the payment of a price for the use of a sum lent in addition to the repayment of the sum itself, was in all cases prohibited. The fact that the payment demanded was moderate was irrelevant; there could be no question of the reasonableness of the amount of an essentially unjust payment.[1] Nor was the payment of usury rendered just because the loan was for a productive purpose—in other words, a commercial loan. Certain writers have maintained that in this case usury was tolerated;[2] but they can easily be refuted. As we have seen above, *mutuum* was essentially a sale, and, therefore, no additional price could be charged because of some special individual advantage enjoyed by the buyer (or borrower). It was quite impossible to distinguish, according to the scholastic teaching, between taking an additional payment because the lender made a profit by using the loan wisely, and taking it because the borrower was in great distress, and therefore derived a greater advantage from the loan than a person in easier circumstances. The erroneous notion that loans for productive purposes were entitled to any special treatment was finally dispelled in 1745 by an encyclical of Benedict XIV.[3]

[1] Jourdain, *op. cit.*, p. 35.

[2] *E.g.* Périn, *Premiers Principes d'Économie politique*, p. 305; Claudio Jannet, *Capital Spéculation et Finance*, p. 83; De Metz-Noblat, *Lois économiques*, p. 293.

[3] Rambaud, *op. cit.*, p. 69.

§ 5. *Extrinsic Titles*

Usury, therefore, was prohibited in all cases. Many people at the present day think that the prohibition of usury was the same thing as the prohibition of interest. There could not be a greater mistake. While usury was in all circumstances condemned, interest was in every case allowed. The justification of interest rested on precisely the same ground as the prohibition of usury, namely, the observance of the equality of commutative justice. It was unjust that a greater price should be paid for the loan of a sum of money than the amount lent ; but it was no less unjust that the lender should find himself in a worse position because of his having made the loan. In other words, the consideration for the loan could not be increased because of any special benefit which it conferred on the borrower, but it could be increased on account of any special damage suffered by the lender—precisely the same rule as we have seen applied in the case of sales. The borrower must, in addition to the repayment of the loan, indemnify the lender for any damage he had suffered. The measure of the damage was the difference between the lender's condition before the loan was made and after it had been repaid—in other words, he was entitled to compensation for the difference in his condition occasioned by the transaction—*id quod interest.*

Before we discuss interest properly so called, we must say a word about another analogous but not identical title of compensation, namely, the *poena conventionalis.* It was a very general practice, about the legitimacy of which the scholastics do not seem to have had any doubt, to attach to the original contract of loan an agreement that a penalty should be paid in case of default in the repayment of the loan at the stipulated time.[1] The justice of the *poena conventionalis* was recognised by Alexander of Hales,[2] and by Duns Scotus, who gives a typical form of the stipulation as follows : ' I have need of my money for commerce, but shall lend it to you till a certain day on the condition that, if you do not repay it on that day, you shall pay me afterwards a certain sum in addition, since I shall suffer much injury through your delay.' [3] The *poena conventionalis* must not be confused with either of the titles *damnum emergens* or *lucrum cessans,* which we are about to discuss ; it was distinguished from the former by being based upon a presumed injury, whereas the injury in *damnum emergens* must be proved ; and for the latter because the damage must be presumed to have occurred after the expiration of the loan period, whereas in *lucrum cessans* the damage was presumed to have occurred during the currency of the loan period. The important thing to remember is that these titles were really distinct.[4] The essentials of a *poena conventionalis* were, stipulation from the first day of the loan, presumption

[1] Ashley, *op. cit.,* vol. i. pt. i. p. 399.
[2] Biel, *op. cit.,* iv. 15, 11.   [3] Cleary, *op. cit.,* p. 93.
[4] *Ibid.,* p. 95.

of damage, and attachment to a loan which was itself gratuitous.[1] The *Summa Astesana* clearly maintained the distinction between the two titles of compensation,[2] as also did the *Summa Angelica*.[3]

The first thing to be noted on passing from the *poena conventionalis* to interest proper is that the latter ground of compensation was generally divided into two kinds, *damnum emergens* and *lucrum cessans*. The former included all cases where the lender had incurred an actual loss by reason of his having made the loan ; whereas the latter included all cases where the lender, by parting with his money, had lost the opportunity of making a profit. This distinction was made at least as early as the middle of the thirteenth century, and was always adopted by later writers.[4]

The title *damnum emergens* never presented any serious difficulty. It was recognised by Albertus Magnus,[5] and laid down so clearly by Aquinas that it was not afterwards questioned : ' A lender may without sin enter an agreement with the borrower for compensation for the loss he incurs of something he ought to have, for this is not to sell the use of money, but to avoid a loss. It may also happen that the borrower avoids a greater loss than the lender incurs, wherefore the borrower may repay the lender with what he has gained.' [6] The usual example given to illustrate how *damnum emergens* might arise, was the

[1] Cleary, *op. cit.*, p. 94.
[2] Endemann, *Studien*, vol. i. p. 20.   [3] ccxl.
[4] Ashley, *op. cit.*, vol. i. pt. ii. p. 399.
[5] Roscher, *Geschichte*, p. 27.   [6] II. ii. 78, 2, ad. 1.

case of the lender being obliged, on account of the failure of the borrower, to borrow money himself at usury.[1]

Closely allied to the title of *damnum emergens* was that of *lucrum cessans.* According to some writers, the latter was the only true interest. Dr. Cleary quotes some thirteenth-century documents in which a clear distinction is made between *damnum* and *interesse* ; [2] and it seems to have been the common custom in Germany at a later date to distinguish between *interesse* and *schaden.*[3] Although the division between these two titles was very indefinite, they did not meet recognition with equal readiness; the title *damnum emergens* was universally admitted by all authorities; while that of *lucrum cessans* was but gradually admitted, and hedged round with many limitations.[4]

The first clear recognition of the title *lucrum cessans* occurs in a letter from Alexander III., written in 1176, and addressed to the Archbishop of Genoa : ' You ' tell us that it often happens in your city that people buy pepper and cinnamon and other wares, at the time worth not more than five pounds, promising those from whom they

---

[1] Ashley, *op. cit.*, vol. i. pt. i. p. 400. [2] *Op. cit.*, p. 95.

[3] Ashley, *op. cit.*, vol. i. pt. ii. p. 401.

[4] Cleary, *op. cit.*, p. 98 ; Endemann, *Studien*, vol. ii. p. 279 ; Bartolus and Baldus said that *damnum emergens* and *lucrum cessans* were divided by a very narrow line, and that it was often difficult to distinguish between them. They suggested that the terms *interesse proximum* and *interesse remotum* would be more satisfactory, but they were not followed by other writers (Endemann, *Studien*, vol. ii. pp. 269-70).

received them six pounds at an appointed time. Though contracts of this kind and under such a form cannot strictly be called usurious, yet, nevertheless, the vendors incur guilt, unless they are really doubtful whether the wares might be worth more or less at the time of payment. Your citizens will do well for their own salvation to cease from such contracts.'[1] As Dr. Cleary points out, the trader is held by this decision to be entitled to a recompense on account of a probable loss of profit, and the decision consequently amounts to a recognition of the title *lucrum cessans*.[2] The title is also recognised by Scotus and Hostiensis.[3]

The attitude of Aquinas to the admission of *lucrum cessans* is obscure. In the article on usury he expressly states that ' the lender cannot enter an agreement for compensation through the fact that he makes no profit out of his money, because he must not sell that which he has not yet, and may be prevented in many ways from having.'[4] Two comments must be made on this passage ; first, that it only refers to making a stipulation in advance for compensation for profit lost, and does not condemn the actual payment of compensation ;[5] second, that the point is made that the probability of gaining a profit on money is so problematical as to make it unsaleable. As Ashley points out, the latter consideration was peculiarly important at the time when the *Summa*

---

[1] *Decr. Greg.* v. 5, 6.   [2] *Op. cit.*, p. 67.
[3] *Ibid.*, p. 99.   [4] II. ii. 78, 2, ad. 1.
[5] Rambaud, *op. cit.*, p. 67.

was composed ; and, when in the course of the following two centuries the opportunities for reasonably safe and profitable business investments increased, the great theologians conceived that they were following the real thought of Aquinas by giving to this explanation a pure *contemporanea expositio.* The argument in favour of this construction is strengthened by a reference to the article of the *Summa* dealing with restitution,[1] where it is pointed out that a man may suffer in two ways—first, by being deprived of what he actually has, and, second, by being prevented from obtaining what he was on his way to obtain. In the former case an equivalent must always be restored, but in the latter it is not necessary to make good an equivalent, ' because to have a thing virtually is less than to have it actually, and to be on the way to obtain a thing is to have it merely virtually or potentially, and so, were he to be indemnified by receiving the thing actually, he would be paid, not the exact value taken from him, but more, and this is not necessary for salvation. However, he is bound to make some compensation according to the condition of persons and things.' Later in the same article we are told that ' he that has money has the profit not actually, but only virtually ; and it may be hindered in many ways.' [2] It seems quite clear from these passages that Aquinas admitted the right to compensation for a profit which the lender was hindered from making on account of the loan ; but that, in the circumstances of the time, the

[1] II. ii. 62, 4.   [2] *Ibid.*, ad. 1 and 2.

probability of making such a profit was so remote that it could not be made the basis of pecuniary compensation. The probability of there being a *lucrum cessans* was thought small, but the justice of its reward, if it did in fact exist, was admitted.

This interpretation steadily gained ground amongst succeeding writers ; so that, in spite of some lingering opposition, the justice of the title *lucrum cessans* was practically universally admitted by the theologians of the fifteenth century.[1]

Of course the burden of proving that an opportunity for profitable investment had been really lost was on the lender, but this onus was sufficiently discharged if the probability of such a loss were established. In the fifteenth century, with the expansion of commerce, it came to be generally recognised that such a probability could be presumed in the case of the merchant or trader.[2] The final condition of this development of the teaching on *lucrum cessans* is thus stated by Ashley : [3] ' Any merchant, or indeed any person in a trading centre where there were opportunities of business investment (outside money-lending itself) could, with a perfectly clear conscience, and without any fear of molestation, contract to receive periodical interest from the person to whom he lent money ; *provided only* that he first lent it to him gratuitously, for a period that might be made very short, so that technically the pay-

---

[1] Ashley, *op. cit.*, p. 99. *Lucrum cessans* was defined by Navarrus as ' amissio facta a creditore per pecuniam sibi non redditam ' (Endemann, *Studien*, vol. ii. p. 279).

[2] Ashley, *op. cit.*, vol. i. pt. ii. p. 402.   [3] *Ibid.*

ment would not be reward for the use, but compensation for the non-return of the money.' At a later period than that of which we are treating in the present essay the short gratuitous period could be dispensed with, but until the end of the fifteenth century it seems to have been considered essential.[1]

Of course the amount paid in respect of *lucrum cessans* must be reasonable in regard to the loss of opportunity actually experienced; 'Lenders,' says Buridan, ' must not take by way of *lucrum cessans* more than they would have actually made by commerce or in exchange ' ;[2] and Ambrosius de Vignate explains that compensation must only be made for ' the time and just *interesse* of the lost gain, which must be certain and proximate.'[3]

There was another title on account of which more than the amount of the loan could be recovered, namely, *periculum sortis*. In one sense it was a contradiction in terms to speak of the element of risk in connection with usury, because from its very definition usury was gain without risk as opposed to profit from a trading partnership, which, as we shall see presently, consisted of gain coupled with the risk of loss. It could not be lost sight of, however, that in fact there might be a risk of the loan not being repaid through the insolvency of the borrower, or some other cause, and the question arose whether the lender could justly claim any compensation for

[1] Ashley, *op. cit.*, vol. i. pt. ii. p. 402 ; Endemann, *Studien*, vol. ii. pp. 253-4 ; Cleary, *op. cit.*, p. 100.
[2] *Eth.*, iv. 6.   [3] *De Usuris*, c. 10.

the undertaking of this risk. ' Regarded as an extrinsic title, risk of losing the principal is connected with the contract of *mutuum*, and entitles the lender to some compensation for running the risk of losing his capital in order to oblige a possibly insolvent debtor. The greater the danger of insolvency, the greater naturally would be the charge. The contract was indifferent to the object of the loan ; it mattered not whether it was intended for commerce or consumption ; it was no less indifferent to profit on the part of the borrower ; it took account simply of the latter's ability to pay, and made its charge accordingly. It resembled consequently the contracts made by insurance companies, wherein there is a readiness to risk the capital sum for a certain rate of payment ; the only difference was that the probabilities charged for were not so much the likelihood of having to pay, as the likelihood of not receiving back.' [1]

We have referred above, when dealing with the legitimacy of commercial profits, to the difficulty which was felt in admitting the justice of compensation for risk, on account of the Gregorian Decretal on the subject. The same decree gave rise to the same difficulty in connection with the justification of a recompense for *periculum sortis*. There was a serious dispute about the actual wording of the decree, and even those who agreed as to its wording differed as to its interpretation.[2] The justice of the title was, however, admitted by Scotus, who said that it was lawful to stipulate

[1] Cleary, *op. cit.*, p. 115.   [2] *Ibid.*

for recompense when both the principal and
surplus were in danger of being lost [1]; by Carletus; [2] and by Nider. [3] The question, however,
was still hotly disputed at the end of the fifteenth
century, and was finally settled in favour of the
admission of the title as late as 1645. [4]

§ 6. *Other Cases in which more than the Loan could be repaid*

We have now discussed the extrinsic titles—
*poena conventionalis, damnum emergens, lucrum
cessans,* and *periculum sortis.* There were other
grounds also, which cannot be reduced to the
classification of extrinsic titles, on which more
than the amount of the loan might be justly
returned to the lender. In the first place, the
lender might justly receive anything that the
borrower chose to pay over and above the loan,
voluntarily as a token of gratitude. ' Repayment for a favour may be done in two ways,' says
Aquinas. ' In one way, as a debt of justice ; and
to such a debt a man may be bound by a fixed
contract ; and its amount is measured according
to the favour received. Wherefore the borrower
of money, or any such thing the use of which is its
consumption, is not bound to repay more than he
received in loan ; and consequently it is against
justice if he is obliged to pay back more. In
another way a man's obligation to repayment for
favour received is based on a debt of friendship,

---

[1] Cleary, *op. cit.*, p. 117.   [2] *Summa Angelica Usura,* i. 38.
[3] *De Cont. Merc.*, iii. 15.   [4] Cleary, *op. cit.*, p. 117.

and the nature of this debt depends more on the
feeling with which the favour was conferred than
on the question of the favour itself. This debt
does not carry with it a civil obligation, involving
a kind of necessity that would exclude the spontaneous nature of such a repayment.' [1]

It was also clearly understood that it was not
wrongful to borrow at usury under certain conditions. In such cases the lender might commit
usury in receiving, but the borrower would not
commit usury in paying an amount greater than
the sum lent. It was necessary, however, in
order that borrowing at usury might be justified,
that the borrower should be animated by some
good motive, such as the relief of his own or
another's need. The whole question was settled
once and for all by Aquinas : ' It is by no means
lawful to induce a man to sin, yet it is lawful to
make use of another's sin for a good end, since even
God uses all sin for some good, since He draws
some good from every evil. . . . Accordingly it
is by no means lawful to induce a man to lend
under a condition of usury ; yet it is lawful to
borrow for usury from a man who is ready to do
so, and is a usurer by profession, provided that
the borrower have a good end in view, such as the
relief of his own or another's need. . . . He who
borrows for usury does not consent to the usurer's
sin, but makes use of it. Nor is it the usurer's
acceptance of usury that pleases him, but his
lending, which is good.' [2]

We should mention here the *montes pietatis,*

[1] II. ii. 78, 2, ad. 2.   [2] II. ii. 78, 4.

which occupied a prominent place among the
credit-giving agencies of the later Middle Ages,
although it is difficult to say whether their methods
were examples of or exceptions to the doctrines
forbidding usury. These institutions were formed
on the model of the *montes profani*, the system of
public debt resorted to by many Italian States.
Starting in the middle of the twelfth century,[1]
the Italian States had recourse to forced loans
in order to raise reserves for extraordinary necessities, and, in order to prevent the growth of
disaffection among the citizens, an annual percentage on such loans was paid. A fund raised
by such means was generally called a *mons* or heap.
The propriety of the payment of this percentage
was warmly contested during the fourteenth and
fifteenth centuries—the Dominicans and Franciscans defending it, and the Augustinians attacking
it. But its justification was not difficult. In the
first place, the loans were generally, if not universally, forced, and therefore the payment of
interest on them was purely voluntary. As we
have seen, Aquinas was quite clear as to the
lawfulness of such a voluntary payment. In
the second place, the lenders were almost invari-
ably members of the trading community, who were
the very people in whose favour a recompense for
lucrum cessans would be allowed.[2] Laurentius de
Rodulphis argued in favour of the justice of these
State loans, and contended that the bondholders
were entitled to sell their rights, but advised good

---

[1] Endemann, *Studien*, vol. i. p. 433.
[2] Ashley, *op. cit.*, vol. i. pt. i. p. 448.

Christians to abstain from the practice of a right about the justice of which theologians were in such disagreement [1]; and Antoninus of Florence, who was in general so strict on the subject of usury, took the same view.[2]

It was probably the example of these State loans, or *montes profani*, that suggested to the Franciscans the possibility of creating an organisation to provide credit facilities for poor borrowers, which was in many ways analogous to the modern co-operative credit banks. Prior to the middle of the fifteenth century, when this experiment was initiated, there had been various attempts by the State to provide credit facilities for the poor, but these need not detain us here, as they did not come to anything.[3] The first of the *montes pietatis* was founded at Orvieto by the Franciscans in 1462, and after that year they spread rapidly.[4] The *montes*, although their aim was exclusively philanthropic, found themselves obliged to make a small charge to defray their working expenses, and, although one would think that this could be amply justified by the title of *damnum emergens*, it provoked a violent attack by the Dominicans. The principal antagonist of the *montes pietatis* was Thomas da Vio, who wrote a special treatise on the subject, in which he made the point that

---

[1] *De Usuris.*   [2] Ashley, *op. cit.*, p. 449.
[3] Cleary, *op. cit.*, p. 108 ; Brants, *op. cit.*, p. 159.
[4] Perugia, 1467 ; Viterbo, 1472 ; Sevona, 1472 ; Assisi, 1485 ; Mantua, 1486 ; Cesana and Parma, 1488 ; Interamna and Lucca, 1489 ; Verona, 1490 ; Padua, 1491, etc. (Endemann, *Studien*, vol. i. p. 463).

the *montes* charged interest from the very beginning of the loan, which was a contradiction of all the previous teaching on interest.[1]

The general feeling of the Church, however, was in favour of the *montes*. It was felt that, if the poor must borrow, it was better that they should borrow at a low rate of interest from philanthropic institutions than at an extortionate rate from usurers; several *montes* were established under the direct protection of the Popes;[2] and finally, in 1515, the Lateran Council gave an authoritative judgment in favour of the *montes*. This decree contains an excellent definition of usury as it had come to be accepted at that date: ' Usury is when gain is sought to be acquired from the use of a thing, not fruitful in itself, without labour, expense, or risk on the part of the lender.'[3]

It was generally admitted by the theologians that the taking of usury might be permitted by the civil authorities, although it was insisted that acting in accordance with this permission did not absolve the conscience of the usurer. Albertus Magnus conceded that ' although usury is contrary to the perfection of Christian laws, it is at least not contrary to civil interests ';[4] and Aquinas also justified the toleration of usury by the State: ' Human laws leave certain things unpunished, on account of the condition of those who are imperfect, and who would be deprived of many advantages if all sins were strictly forbidden

[1] *De Monte Pietatis.* [2] Cleary, *op. cit.*, p. 111.
[3] Ashley, *op. cit.*, vol. i. pt. ii. p. 451.
[4] Rambaud, *op. cit.*, p. 65 ; Espinas, *op. cit.*, p. 103.

and punishments appointed for them.   Wherefore
human law has permitted usury, not that it looks
upon usury as harmonising with justice, but lest
the advantage of many should be hindered.' [1]
Although   this   opinion   was   controverted   by
Ægidius Romanus,[2] it was generally accepted
by later writers. Thus Gerson says that ' the
civil law, when it tolerates usury in some cases,
must not be said to be always contrary to the law
of God or the Church.   The civil legislator, acting
in the manner of a wise doctor, tolerates lesser
evils that greater ones may be avoided.   It is
obviously less of an evil that slight usury should
be permitted for the relief of want, than that men
should be driven by their want to rob or steal,
or to sell their goods at an unfairly low price.' [3]
Buridan explains that the attitude of the State
towards usury must never be more than one of
toleration ; it must not actively approve of usury,
but it may tacitly refuse to punish it.[4]

§ 7. *The Justice of Unearned Income*

Many modern socialists—'Christian' and otherwise—have asserted that the teaching of the
Church on usury was a pronouncement in favour
of the unproductivity of capital.[5] Thus Rudolf
Meyer, one of the most distinguished of ' Christian
socialists,' has argued that if one recognises the
productivity of land or stock, one must also recog-

[1] II. ii. 78, 1, ad. 3.   [2] *De Reg. Prin.*, ii. 3, 11.
[3] *De Cont.*, ii. 17.   [4] *Quaest. super. Lib. Eth.*, iv. 6.
[5] Ashley, *op. cit.*, vol. i. pt. ii. p. 427.

nise the productivity of money, and that therefore the Church, in denying the productivity of the
latter, would be logically driven to deny the productivity of the former.[1]   Anton Menger expresses
the same opinion : ' There is not the least reason
for attacking from the moral and religious stand-
points loans at interest and usury more than any
other form of unearned income. If one questions
the legitimacy of loans at interest, one must
equally condemn as inadmissible the other forms
of profit from capital and lands, and particularly
the feudal institutions of the Middle Ages. . . .
It would have been but a logical consequence for
the Church to have condemned all forms of unearned revenue.' [2]

No such conclusion, however, can be properly
drawn from the mediæval teaching. The whole
discussion on usury turned on the distinction
which was drawn between things of which the use
could be transferred without the ownership, and
things of which the use could not be so transferred.
In the former category were placed all things
which could be used, either by way of enjoyment
or employment for productive purposes, without
being destroyed in the process ; and in the latter
all things of which the use or employment involved
the destruction.

With regard to income derived from the former,
no difficulty was ever felt ; a farm or a house
might be let at a rent without any question, the

---

[1] *Der Kapitalismus fin de siècle*, p. 29.

[2] *Das Recht auf den Arbeiterstrag.* See the Abbé Hohoff in *Démocratie Chrétienne*, Sept. 1898, p. 284.

return received being universally regarded as one of the legitimate fruits of the ownership of the thing. With regard to the latter, however, a difficulty did arise, because it was felt that a so-called loan of such goods was, when analysed, in reality a sale, and that therefore any increase which the goods produced was in reality the property, not of the lender, but of the borrower. That money was in all cases sterile was never suggested ; on the contrary, it was admitted that it might produce a profit if wisely and prudently employed in industry or commerce ; but it was felt that such an increase, when it took place, was the rightful property of the owner of the money. But when money was lent, the owner of this money was the borrower, and therefore, when money which was lent was employed in such a way as to produce a profit, that profit belonged to the borrower, not the lender. In this way the schoolmen were strictly logical ; they fully admitted that wealth could produce wealth ; but they insisted that that additional wealth should accrue to the owner of the wealth that produced it.

The fact is, as Böhm-Bawerk has pointed out, that the question of the productivity of capital was never discussed by the mediæval schoolmen, for the simple reason that it was so obvious. The justice of receiving an income from an infungible thing which was temporarily lent by its owner, was discussed and supported ; but the justice of the owner of such a thing receiving an income from the thing so long as it remained in his own possession was never discussed, because it was uni-

versally admitted.[1] It is perfectly correct to say
that the problems which have perplexed modern
writers as to the justice of receiving an unearned
income from one's property never occurred to
the scholastics ; such problems can only arise
when the institution of private property comes
to be questioned ; and private property was
the keystone of the whole scholastic economic
conception.   In other words, the justice of a
reward for capital was admitted because it was
unquestioned.

The question that caused difficulty was whether
money could be considered a form of capital.   At
the present day, when the opportunities of industrial investment are wider than they ever
were before, the principal use to which money is
put is the financing of industrial enterprises ; but
in the Middle Ages this was not the case, precisely
because the opportunities of profitable investment
were so few.   This is the reason why the mediæval writers did not find it necessary to discuss in
detail the rights of the owner of money who used
it for productive purposes.   But of the justice of
a profit being reaped when money was actually
so employed there was no doubt at all.   As we
have seen, the borrower of a sum of money might
reap a profit from its wise employment ; there
was no question about the justice of taking such
a profit ; and the only matter in dispute was
whether that profit should belong to the borrower
or the lender of the money.   This dispute was
decided in favour of the borrower on the ground

[1] *Capital and Interest*, p. 39.

that, according to the true nature of the contract of *mutuum,* the money was his property. It was, therefore, never doubted that even money might produce a profit for its owner. The only difference between infungible goods and money was that, in the case of the former, the use might be transferred apart from the property, whereas, in the case of the latter, it could not be so transferred.

The recognition of the title *lucrum cessans* as a ground for remuneration clearly implies the recognition of the legitimacy of the owner of money deriving a profit from its use ; and the slowness of the scholastics to admit this title was precisely because of the rarity of opportunities for so employing money in the earlier Middle Ages. The nature of capital was clearly understood ; but the possibility of money constituting capital arose only with the extension of commerce and the growth of profitable investments. Those scholastics who strove to abolish or to limit the recognition of *lucrum cessans* as a ground for remuneration did not deny the productivity of capital, but simply thought the money had not at that time acquired the characteristics of capital.[1]

If there were any doubt about the fact that the scholastics recognised the legitimacy of unearned income, it would be dispelled by an understanding of their teaching on rents and partnership, in the former of which they distinctly acknowledged the right to draw an unearned income from one's

[1] See Ashley, *op. cit.,* vol. i. pt. ii. pp. 434-9.

land, and in the latter of which they acknowledged the same right in regard to one's money.[1]

§ 8. *Rent Charges*

There was never any difficulty about admitting the justice of receiving a rent from a tenant in occupation of one's lands, because land was understood to be essentially a thing of which the use could be sold apart from the ownership ; and it was also recognised that the recipient of such a rent might sell his right to a third party, who could then demand the rent from the tenant. When this was admitted it was but a small step to admit the right of the owner of land to create a rent in favour of another person in consideration for some payment. The distinctions between a *census reservativus*, or a rent established when the possession of land was actually transferred to a tenant, and a *census constitutivus*, or a rent created upon property remaining in the possession of the payer, did not become the subject of discussion or difficulty until the sixteenth century.[2] The legitimacy of rent charges does not seem to have been questioned by the theologians ; the best proof of this being the absence of controversy about them in a period when they were undoubtedly very common, especially in Germany.[3] Langen-

---

[1] On this discussion see Ashley, *Economic History*, vol. i. pt. ii. pp. 427 *et seq.* ; Rambaud, *Histoire*, pp. 57 *et seq.* ; Funk, *Zins und Wucher* ; Arnold, *Zur Geschichte des Eigenthums*, pp. 92 *et seq.* ; Böhm-Bawerk, *Capital and Interest* (Eng. trans.), pp. 1-39.

[2] Ashley, *op. cit.*, vol. i. pt. ii. p. 409.

[3] Endemann, *Studien*, vol. ii. p. 104.

stein, whose opinion on the subject was followed
by many later writers,[1] thought that the receipt
of income from rent charges was perfectly justifiable, when the object was to secure a provision
for old age, or to provide an income for persons
engaged in the services of Church or State, but
that it was unjustifiable if it was intended to
enable nobles to live in luxurious idleness, or
plebeians to desert honest toil.   It is obvious that
Langenstein did not regard rent charges as wrongful in themselves, but simply as being the possible
occasions of wrong.[2]

In the fifteenth century definite pronounce-
ments on rent charges were made by the Popes.
A large part of the revenue of ecclesiastical bodies
consisted of rent charges, and in 1425 several
persons in the diocese of Breslau refused to pay
the rents they owed to their clergy on the ground
that they were usurious.   The question was
referred to Pope Martin v., whose bull deciding
the matter was generally followed by all subse-
quent authorities.   The bull decides in favour
of the lawfulness of rent charges, provided certain
conditions were observed.   They must be charged
on fixed property ('super bonis suis, dominiis,
oppidis, terris, agris, praediis, domibus et heredi-
tatibus') and determined beforehand; they must
be moderate, not exceeding seven or ten per cent. ;
and they must be capable of being repurchased at
any moment in whole or in part, by the repayment
of the same sum for which they were originally

<hr/>

[1] Endemann, *Studien*, vol. ii. p. 109.
[2] Roscher, *Geschichte*, p. 20.

created.   On the other hand, the payer of the
rent must never be forced to repay the purchase
money, even if the goods on which the rent was
charged had perished—in other words, the contract creating the rent charge was one of sale, and
not of loan.   The bull recites that such conditions
had been observed in contracts of this nature
from time immemorial.[1]   A precisely similar
decree was issued by Calixtus III. in 1455.[2]

These decisions were universally followed in the
fifteenth century.[3]   It was always insisted that
a rent could only be charged upon something of
which the use could be separated from the ownership, as otherwise it would savour of usury.[4]   In
the sixteenth century interesting discussions arose
about the possibility of creating a personal rent
charge, not secured on any specific property, but
such discussions did not trouble the writers of the
period which we are treating.   The only instance
of such a contract being considered is found in
a bull of Nicholas V. in 1452, permitting such
personal rent charges in the kingdoms of Aragon
and Sicily, but this permission was purely local,
and, as the bull itself shows, was designed to meet
the exigencies of a special situation.[5]

§ 9. *Partnership*

The teaching on partnership contains such a
complete disproof of the contention that the

---

[1] *Extrav. Commun.*, iii. 5, i.   [2] *Ibid.*, c. 2.
[3] Ashley, *op. cit.*, vol. i. pt. ii. p. 410.
[4] Biel, *op. cit.*, Sent. IV. xv. 12.   [5] Cleary, *op. cit.*, p. 124.

mediæval teaching on usury was based on the unproductivity of capital, that certain writers have endeavoured to prove that the permission of partnership was but a subterfuge, consciously designed to justify evasions of the usury law. Further historical knowledge, however, has dispelled this misconception ; and it is now certain that the contract of partnership was widely practised and tolerated long before the Church attempted to insist on the observance of its usury laws in everyday commercial life.[1] However interesting an investigation into the commercial and industrial partnerships of the Middle Ages might be, we must not attempt to pursue it here, as we have rigidly limited ourselves to a consideration of teaching. We must refer, however, to the *commenda*, which was the contract from which the later mediæval partnership (*societas*) is generally admitted to have developed, because the *commenda* was extensively practised as early as the tenth century, and, as far as we know, never provoked any expression of disapproval from the Church. This silence amounts to a justification ; and we may therefore say that, even before Aquinas devoted his attention to the subject, the Church fully approved of an institution which provided the owner of money with the means of procuring an unearned income.

The *commenda* was originally a contract by which merchants who wished to engage in foreign trade, but who did not wish to travel themselves,

[1] Ashley, *op. cit.*, vol. i. pt. ii. p. 411 ; Weber, *Handelsgesellschaften*, pp. 111-14.

entrusted their wares to agents or representatives. The merchant was known as the *commendator* or *socius stans*, and the agent as the *commendatarius* or *tractator*. The most usual arrangement for the division of the profits of the adventure was that the *commendatarius* should receive one-fourth and the *commendator* three-fourths. At a slightly later date contracts came to be common in which the *commendatarius* contributed a share of capital, in which case he would receive one-fourth of the whole profit as *commendatarius*, and a proportionate share of the remainder as capitalist. This contract came to be generally known as *collegantia* or *societas*. Contracts of this kind, though originally chiefly employed in overseas enterprise, afterwards came to be utilised in internal trade and manufacturing industry.[1]

The legitimacy of the profits of the *commendator* never seems to have caused the slightest difficulty to the canonists. In 1206 Innocent III. advised the Archbishop of Genoa that a widow's dowry should be entrusted to some merchant so that an income might be obtained by means of honest gain.[2] Aquinas expressly distinguishes between profit made from entrusting one's money to a merchant to be employed by him in trade, and profit arising from a loan, on the ground that in the former case the ownership of the money does not pass, and that therefore the person who derives the profit also risks the loan. 'He who lends money transfers the ownership of the money

[1] Ashley, *op. cit.*, vol. i. pt. ii. pp. 412-14.
[2] *Greg. Decr.*, iv. 19, 7.

to the borrower.   Hence the borrower holds the money at his own risk, and is bound to pay it all back : wherefore the lender must not exact more. On the other hand, he that entrusts his money to a merchant or craftsman so as to form a kind of society does not transfer the ownership of the money to them, for it remains his, so that at his risk the merchant speculates with it, or the craftsman uses it for his craft, and consequently he may lawfully demand, as something belonging to him, part of the profits derived from his money.' [1] This dictum of Aquinas was the foundation of all the later teaching on partnership, and the importance of the element of risk was insisted on in strong terms by the later writers.   According to Baldus, ' when there is no sharing of risk there is no partnership ' ; [2] and Paul de Castro says, ' A partnership when the gain is shared, but not the loss, is not to be permitted.' [3] ' The legitimacy,' says Brants, ' of the contract of *commenda* always rested upon the same principle ; capital could not be productive except for him who worked it himself, or who caused it to be worked on his own responsibility.   This latter condition was realised in *commenda*.' [4]

Although the contract of partnership was fully recognised by the scholastics, it was not very scientifically treated, nor were the different species of the contract systematically classified.   The only classification adopted was to divide contracts of

---

[1] II. ii. 78, 2, ad. 5.   [2] Brants, *op. cit.*, p. 167.

[3] *Consilia*, ii. 55 ; also Ambrosius de Vignate, *De Usuris*, i. 62 ; Biel, *op. cit.*, IV. xv. 11.   [4] *Op. cit.*, p. 172.

partnership into two kinds—those where both parties contributed labour to a joint enterprise, and those where one party contributed labour and the other party money. The former gave no difficulty, because the justice of the remuneration of labour was admitted; but, while the latter was no less fully recognised, cases of it were subjected to careful scrutiny, because it was feared that usurious contracts might be concealed under the appearance of a partnership.[1] The question which occupied the greatest space in the treatises on the subject was the share in which the profits should be divided between the parties. The only rule which could be laid down, in the absence of an express contract, was that the parties should be remunerated in proportion to the services which they contributed—a rule the application of which must have been attended with enormous difficulties. Laurentius de Rodulphis insists that equality must be observed;[2] and Angelus de Periglis de Perusio, the first monographist on the subject, does not throw much more light on the question. The rule as stated by this last writer is that in the first place the person contributing money must be repaid a sum equal to what he put in, and the person contributing labour must be paid a sum equal to the value of his labour, and that whatever surplus remains must be divided between the two parties equally.[3] The question of the shares in which the profits should be distributed was not one, however, that

---

[1] *Summa Astesana*, iii. 12.   [2] *De Usuris*, i. 19.

[3] *De Societatibus*, i. 130.

frequently arose in practice, because it was the almost universal custom for the partners to make this a term of their original contract. Within fairly wide limits it was possible to arrange for the division of the profits in unequal shares—say two-thirds and one-third. The shares of gain and loss must, however, be the same ; one party could not reap two-thirds of the profit and bear only one-third of the loss ; but it might be contracted that, when the loss was deducted from the gain, one party might have two-thirds of the balance, and the other one-third.[1] In no case, of course, could the party contributing the money stipulate that his principal should in all cases be returned, because that was a *mutuum*. The party contributing the labour might validly contract that he should be paid for his labour in any case, but, if this was so, the contract ceased to be a *societas* and became a *locatio operarum*, or ordinary contract of work for wages. In all cases, common participation in the gains and losses of the enterprise was an essential feature of the contract of partnership.[2]

Before concluding the subject of partnership, we must make reference to the *trinus contractus*, which caused much discussion and great difficulty. As we have seen, a contract of partnership was good so long as the person contributing money did not contract that he should receive his original money back in all circumstances. A contract of insurance was equally justifiable. There was no doubt that A might enter into partnership with

[1] *De Societatibus*, i. 130.   [2] *Ibid.*

B ; he could further insure himself with C against the loss of his capital, and with D against damage caused by fluctuations in the rate of profits. Why, then, should he not simultaneously enter into all three contracts with B ? If he did so, he was still B's partner, but at the same time he was protected against the loss of his principal and a fair return upon it—in other words, he was a partner, protected against the risks of the enterprise. The legitimacy of such a contract—the *trinus contractus*, as it was called—was maintained by Carletus in the *Summa Angelica*, which was published about 1476, and by Biel.[1] Early in the sixteenth century Eck, a young professor at Ingolstadt, brought the question of the legitimacy of this contract before the University of Bologna, but no formal decision was pronounced, and, had it not been for the reaction following the Reformation, the *trinus contractus* would probably have gained general acceptance. As it was, it was condemned by a provincial synod at Milan in 1565, and by Sixtus v. in 1585.[2]

We should also refer to the contract of bottomry, which consisted of a loan made to the owner—or in some cases the master—of a ship, on the security of the ship, to be repaid with interest upon the safe conclusion of a voyage. This contract could not be considered a partnership, in-

---

[1] *Op. cit.*, iv. xv. 11. Lecky attributed the invention of the *trinus contractus* to the Jesuits—who were only founded in 1534 (*History of Rationalism*, vol. ii. p. 267).

[2] Ashley, *op. cit.*, vol. i. pt. ii. pp. 439 *et seqq.* ; Cleary, *op. cit.*, pp. 126 *et seqq.*

asmuch as the property in the money passed to
the borrower ; but it probably escaped condemnation as usurious on the ground that the lender
shared in the risk of the enterprise. The payment
of some additional sum over and above the money
lent might thus be justified on the ground of *periculum sortis.* The contract, moreover, was really
one of insurance for the shipowner, and contracts
of insurance were clearly legitimate. In any
event the legitimacy of loans on bottomry was
not questioned before the sixteenth century.[1]

§ 10. *Concluding Remarks on Usury*

It is to be hoped that the above exposition of
the mediæval doctrine on usury will dispel the idea
that the doctrine was founded upon the injustice
of unearned income. Far from the receipt of an
unearned income from money or other capital
being in all cases condemned, it was unanimously
recognised, provided that the income accrued to
the owner of the capital, and not to somebody else,
and that the rate of remuneration was just. The
teaching on partnership rested on the fundamental
assumption that a man might trade with his money,
either by using it himself, or by allowing other
people to use it on his behalf. In the latter case,
the person making use of the money might be
either assured of being paid a fixed remuneration
for his services, in which case the contract was one

---

[1] Ashley, *op. cit.*, vol. i. pt. ii. pp. 421-3 ; Palgrave, *Dictionary of
Political Economy*, art. ' Bottomry ' ; Cunningham, *Growth of English
Industry and Commerce*, vol. i. p. 257.

of *locatio operarum*, or he might be willing to let his remuneration depend upon the result of the enterprise, in which case the contract was one of *societas*. In either case the right of the owner of the money to reap a profit from the operation was unquestioned, provided only that he was willing to share the risks of loss. But if, instead of making use of his money for trading either by his own exertions or by those of his partner or agent, he chose to sell his money, he was not permitted to receive more for it than its just price —which was, in fact, the repayment of the same amount. This was what happened in the case of a *mutuum*. In that case the ownership of the money was transferred to the borrower, who was perfectly at liberty to trade with it, if he so desired, and to reap whatever gain that trade produced. The prohibition of usury, far from being proof of the injustice of an income from capital, is proof of quite the contrary, because it was designed to insure that the income from capital should belong to the owner of that capital and to no other person.[1] Although, therefore, no price could be paid for a loan, the lender must be prevented from suffering any damage from making the loan, and he might make good his loss by virtue of the implied collateral contract of indemnity, which we discussed above when treating of extrinsic titles. If the lender, through making the loan, had been prevented from making a profit in trade, he might be indemnified for that loss. All through the discussions on usury we find

[1] See Rambaud, *op. cit.*, p. 59.

express recognition of the justice of the owner of money deriving an income from its employment ; all that the teaching of usury was at pains to define was who the person was to whom money, which was the subject matter of a *mutuum*, belonged. It is quite impossible to comprehend how modern writers can see in the usury teaching of the scholastics a fatal discouragement to the enterprise of traders and capitalists ; and it is equally impossible to understand how socialists can find in that doctrine any suggestion of support for the proposition that all unearned income is immoral and unjust.

Section 3.—The Machinery of Exchange

We have already drawn attention to the fact that there was no branch of economics about which such profound ignorance ruled in the earlier Middle Ages as that of money. As we stated above, even as late as the twelfth century, the theologians were quite content to quote the ill-founded and erroneous opinions of Isidore of Seville as final on the subject. It will be remembered that we also remarked that the question of money was the first economic question to receive systematic scientific treatment from the writers of the later Middle Ages. This remarkable development of opinion on this subject is practically the work of one man, Nicholas Oresme, Bishop of Lisieux, whose treatise, *De Origine, Natura, Jure et Mutationibus Monetarum*, is the earliest example of a pure economic monograph in the modern sense. ' The scholastics,' says Roscher, ' extended their inquiries from the economic point of view further than one is generally disposed to believe ; although it is true that they often did so under a singular form. . . . We can, however, single out Oresme as the greatest scholastic economist for two reasons : on account of the exactitude and clarity of his ideas, and because he succeeded in freeing himself from the pseudo-theological systematisation of things in general, and from the pseudo-philosophical deduction in details.' [1]

Even in the thirteenth century natural economy had not been replaced to any large extent by money economy. The great majority of transactions between man and man were carried on without the intervention of money payments ; and the amount of coin in circulation was consequently small.[2] The question of currency was not therefore one to engage the serious attention of the writers of the time. Aquinas does not deal with money in the *Summa*, except incidentally, and his references to the subject in the *De Regimine Principum*—which occur in the chapters of that work of which the authorship is disputed—simply go to the length of approving Aristotle's opinions on money, and advising the prince to exercise moderation in the exercise of his power of coining *sive in mutando sive in diminuendo pondus*.[3]

---

[1] Quoted in the Introduction to Wolowski's edition of Oresme's *Tractatus* (Paris, 1864).

[2] Brants, *op. cit.*, p. 179 ; Rambaud, *op. cit.*, p. 73.

[3] *De Reg. Prin.*, ii. 13.

As is often the case, the discussion of the rights and duties of the sovereign in connection with the currency only arose when it became necessary for the public to protest against abuses. Philip the Fair of France made it part of his policy to increase the revenue by tampering with the coinage, a policy which was continued by his successors, until it became an intolerable grievance to his subjects. In vain did the Pope thunder against Philip ; [1] in vain did the greatest poet of the age denounce

> ' him that doth work
> With his adulterate money on the Seine.' [2]

Matters continued to grow steadily worse until the middle of the fourteenth century. During the year 1348 there were no less than eleven variations in the value of money in France ; in 1349 there were nine, in 1351 eighteen, in 1353 thirteen, and in 1355 eighteen again. In the course of a single year the value of the silver mark sprang from four to seventeen livres, and fell back again to four. [3] The practice of fixing the price of many necessary commodities must have aggravated the natural evil consequences of such fluctuations. [4]

This grievance had the good result of fixing the attention of scholars on the money question. ' Under the stress of facts and of necessity,' says Brants, ' thinkers applied their minds to the

---

[1] Le Blant, *Traité historique des Monnaies de France*, p. 184.

[2] Dante, *Paradiso*, xix.

[3] Wolowski's Introduction to Oresme's *Tractatus*, p. xxvii.

[4] See Endemann, *Studien*, vol. ii. p. 34.

details of the theory of money, which was the department of economics which, thanks to events, received the earliest illumination. Lawyers, bankers, money-changers, doctors of theology, and publicists of every kind, attached a thoroughly justifiable importance to the question of money. We are no doubt far from knowing all the treatises which saw the light in the fourteenth century upon this weighty question ; but we know enough to affirm that the monetary doctrine was very developed and very far-seeing.' [1] Buridan ana- lysed the different functions and utilities of money, and explained the different ways in which its value might be changed.[2] He did not, however, proceed to discuss the much more important question as to when the sovereign was entitled to make these alterations. This was reserved for Nicholas Oresme, who published his famous treatise about the year 1373. The merits of this work have excited the unanimous admiration of all who have studied it. Roscher says that it contains ' a theory of money, elaborated in the fourteenth century, which remains perfectly correct to-day, under the test of the principles applied in the nineteenth century, and that with a brevity, a precision, a clarity, and a simplicity of language which is a striking proof of the supe- rior genius of its author.' [3] According to Brants, ' the treatise of Oresme is one of the first to be devoted *ex professo* to an economic subject, and

---

[1] *Op. cit.*, p. 186.

[2] *Quaest. super Lib. Eth.*, v. 17 ; *Quaest. super Lib. Pol.*, i. 11.

[3] Quoted in Wolowski, *op. cit.*, and see Roscher, *Geschichte*, p. 25.

it expresses many ideas which are very just, more
just than those which held the field for a long
period after him, under the name of mercantilism,
and more just than those which allowed of the reduction of money as if it were nothing more than
a counter of exchange.' [1]   'Oresme's treatise on
money,' says Macleod, 'may be justly said to
stand at the head of modern economic literature.
This treatise laid the foundations of monetary
science, which are now accepted by all sound
economists.' [2]   'Oresme's completely secular and
naturalistic method of treating one of the most
important problems of political economy,' says
Espinas, 'is a signal of the approaching end of the
Middle Ages and the dawn of the Renaissance.' [3]
Dr. Cunningham adds his tribute of praise : ' The
conceptions of national wealth and national power
were ruling ideas in economic matters for several
centuries, and Oresme appears to be the earliest
of the economic writers by whom they were ex-
plicitly adopted as the very basis of his argument.
. . . A large number of points of economic doctrine
in regard to coinage are discussed with much
judgment and clearness.' [4]   Endemann alone is [5]
inclined to quarrel with the pre-eminence of
Oresme ; but on this question, he is in a minority
of one.[6]

The principal question which Oresme sets out

[1] *Op. cit.*, p. 190.
[2] *History of Economics*, p. 37.   [3] *Op. cit.*, p. 110.
[4] *Growth of English Industry and Commerce*, vol. i. p. 359.
[5] *Grundsätze*, p. 75.
[6] See an interesting note in Brants, *op. cit.*, p. 187.

to answer, according to the first chapter of this treatise, is whether the sovereign has the right to alter the value of the money in circulation at his pleasure, and for his own benefit. He begins the discussion by going over the same ground as Aristotle in demonstrating the origin and utility of money, and then proceeds to discuss the most suitable materials which can be made to serve as money. He decides in favour of gold and silver, and shows himself an unquestioning bimetallist. He further admits the necessity of some token money of small denominations, to be composed of the baser metals. Having drawn attention to the transition from the circulation of money, the value of which is recognised solely by weight, to the circulation of that which is accepted for its imprint or superscription, the author insists that the production of such an imprinted coinage is essentially a matter for the sovereign authority in the State. Oresme now comes to the central point of his thesis. Although, he says, the prince has undoubtedly the power to manufacture and control the coinage, he is by no means the owner of it after it has passed into circulation, because money is a thing which in its essence was invented and introduced in the interests of society as a whole.

Oresme then proceeds to apply this central principle to the solution of the question which he sets himself to answer, and concludes that, as money is essentially a thing which exists for the public benefit, it must not be tampered with, nor varied in value, except in cases of absolute necessity, and in the presence of an un-

controverted general utility. He bases his opposition to unnecessary monetary variation on the
perfectly sound ground that such variation is
productive of loss either to those who are bound
to make or bound to receive fixed sums in payment of obligations. The author then goes on to
analyse the various kinds of variation, which he
says are five—*figurae, proportionis, appellationis,
ponderis,* and *materiae.* Changes of form (*figurae*)
are only justified when it is found that the existing form is liable to increase the damage which
the coins suffer from the wear and tear of usage,
or when the existing currency has been degraded
by widespread illegal coining; changes *proportionis* are only allowable when the relative
value of the different metals constituting the
coinage have themselves changed; simple
changes of name (*appellationis*), such as calling a
mark a pound, are never allowed. Changes of
the weight of the coins (*ponderis*) are pronounced
by Oresme to be just as gross a fraud as the
arbitrary alteration of the weights or measures
by which corn or wine are sold; and changes of
matter (*materiae*) are only to be tolerated when
the supply of the old metal has become insufficient.
The debasement of the coinage by the introduction
of a cheaper alloy is condemned.

In conclusion, Oresme insists that no alteration
of any of the above kinds can be justified at the
mere injunction of the prince ; it must be accomplished *per ipsam communitatem.* The prince
exercises the functions of the community in the
matter of coinage not as *principalis actor,* but as

ordinationis publicae executor. It is pointed out that arbitrary changes in the value of money are really equivalent to a particularly noxious form of taxation ; that they seriously disorganise commerce and impoverish many merchants ; and that the bad coinage drives the good out of circulation. This last observation is of special interest in a fourteenth-century writer, as it shows that Gresham's Law, which is usually credited to a sixteenth-century English economist, was perfectly well understood in the Middle Ages.[1]

This brief account of the ground which Oresme covered, and the conclusions at which he arrived, will enable us to appreciate his importance. Although his clear elucidation of the principles which govern the questions of money was not powerful enough to check the financial abuses of the sovereigns of the later Middle Ages, they exercised a profound influence on the thought of the period, and were accepted by all the theologians of the fifteenth century.[2]

[1] The best edition of Oresme's *Tractatus* is that by Wolowski, published at Paris in 1864, which includes both the Latin and French texts.

[2] Biel, *op. cit.,* IV. xv. 11 ; *De Monetarum Potestate et Utilitate,* referred to in Jourdain, *op. cit.,* p. 34.

CHAPTER IV

CONCLUSION

WE have now passed in review the principal economic doctrines of the mediæval schoolmen. We do not propose to attempt here any detailed criticism of the merits or demerits of the system which we have but briefly sketched. All that we have attempted to do is to present the doctrines in such a way that the reader may be in a position to pass judgment on them. There is one aspect of the subject, however, to which we may be allowed to direct attention before concluding this essay. It is the fashion of many modern writers, especially those hostile to the Catholic Church, to represent the Middle Ages as a period when all scientific advance and economic progress were impeded, if not entirely prevented, by the action of the Church. It would be out of place to inquire into the advances which civilisation achieved in the Middle Ages, as this would lead us into an examination of the whole history of the period ; but we think it well to inquire briefly how far the teaching of the Church on economic matters was calculated to interfere with material progress. This is the lowest standard by which we can judge the mediæval economic teaching, which was essentially aimed at the moral and spiritual elevation of mankind ; but it is a standard which it is worth while to apply, as it is that by which the doctrines of the scholastics have been most generally condemned by modern critics.   To test the mediæval economic doctrine by this, the lowest standard, it may be said that it made for the establishment and development of a rich and prosperous community.   We may summarise the aim of the mediæval teaching by saying that, in the material sphere, it aimed at extended production, wise consumption, and just distribution, which are the chief ends of all economic activity.

It aimed at extended production through its insistence on the importance and dignity of manual labour.[1] As we showed above, one of the principal achievements of Christianity in the social sphere was to elevate labour from a degrading to an honourable occupation. The example of Christ Himself and the Apostles must have made a deep impression on the early Christians; but no less important was the living example to be seen in the monasteries. The part played by the great religious orders in the propagation of this dignified conception cannot be exaggerated. St. Anthony had advised his imitators to busy themselves with meditation, prayer, and the labour of their hands, and had promised that the fear of God would reside in those who laboured at corporal works; and similar exhortations were to be found in the rules of Saints Macarius, Pachomius,

---

[1] See Sabatier, *L'Eglise et le Travail manuel,* and Antoine, *Cours d'Economie sociale,* p. 159.

and Basil.[1]   St. Augustine and St. Jerome recommended that all religious should work for some hours each day with their hands, and a regulation to this effect was embodied in the Rule of St. Benedict.[2] The example of educated and holy men voluntarily taking upon themselves the most menial and tedious employments must have acted as an inspiration to the laity.   The mere economic value of the monastic institutions themselves must have been very great ; agriculture was improved owing to the assiduity and experiments of the monks ; [3] the monasteries were the nurseries of all industrial and artistic progress ; [4] and the example of communities which consumed but a small proportion of what they produced was a striking example to the world of the wisdom and virtue of saving.[5] Not the least of the services which Christian teaching rendered in the domain of production was its insistence upon the dominical repose.[6]

The importance which the scholastics attached to an extended and widespread production is evidenced by their attitude towards the growth of the population.   The fear of over-population does not appear to have occurred to the writers of the

---

[1] Levasseur, *Histoire des Classes ouvrières en France*, vol. i. pp. 182-3.

[2] *Reg. St. Ben.*, c. 48.

[3] List, *National System of Political Economy*, ch. 6.

[4] Janssen, *History of the German People*, vol. ii. p. 2.

[5] *Dublin Review*, N.S., vol. vi. p. 365; see Goyau, *Autour du Catholicisme sociale*, vol. ii. pp. 79-118 ; Gasquet, *Henry VIII. and the English Monasteries*, vol. ii. p. 495.

[6] *Dublin Review*, vol. xxxiii. p. 305.   See Goyau, *Autour du Catholicisme sociale*, vol. ii. pp. 93 *et seq.*

Middle Ages ; [1] on the contrary, a rapidly increasing population was considered a great blessing for a country.[2] This attitude towards the question of population did not arise merely from the fact that Europe was very sparsely populated in the Middle Ages, as modern research has proved that the density of population was much greater than is generally supposed.[3]

The mediæval attitude towards population was founded upon the sanctity of marriage and the respect for human life. The utterances of Aquinas on the subject of matrimony show his keen appreciation of the natural social utility of marriage from the point of view of increasing the population of the world, and of securing that the new generation shall be brought up as good and valuable citizens.[4] While voluntary virginity is recommended as a virtue, it is nevertheless distinctly recognised that the precept of virginity is one which by its very nature can be practised by only a small proportion of the human race, and that it should only be practised by those who seek by detachment from earthly pleasures to regard

[1] Brants, *op. cit.*, p. 235, quoting Sinigaglia, *La Teoria Economica della Populazione in Italia*, Archivio Giuridico, Bologna, 1881.

[2] *Catholic Encyclopædia*, art. 'Population.' Brants draws attention to the interesting fact that a germ of Malthusianism is to be found in the much-discussed *Songe du Vergier*, book ii. chaps. 297-98, and Franciscus Patricius de Senis, writing at the end of the fifteenth century, recommends emigration as the remedy against over-population (*De Institutione Reipublicae*, ix.).

[3] Dureau de la Malle, 'Mémoire sur la Population de la France au xive Siècle,' *Mémoires de l'Académie des Inscriptions et Belles-Lettres*, vol. xiv. p. 36.

[4] *Summa Cont. Gent.*, iii. 123, 136.

divine things.[1] Aquinas further says that large
families help to increase the power of the State,
and deserve well of the commonwealth,[2] and
quotes with approbation the Biblical injunction
to 'increase and multiply.' [3] Ægidius Romanus
demonstrates at length the advantages of large
families in the interests of the family and the
future of the nation.[4]

The growth of a healthy population was made
possible by the reformation of family life, which
was one of the greatest achievements of Christianity in the social sphere.   In the early days of
the Church the institution of the family had been
reconstituted by moderating the harshness of the
Roman domestic rule (*patria potestas*), by raising
the moral and social position of women, and by
reforming the system of testamentary and in-
testate successions ;   and the great importance
which the early Church attached to the family as
the basic unit of social life remained unaltered
throughout the Middle Ages.[5]

The Middle Ages were therefore a period when
the production of wealth was looked upon as a
salutary and honourable vocation.   The wonder-
ful artistic monuments of that era, which have
survived the intervening centuries of decay and
vandalism, are a striking testimony to the perfection of production in a civilisation in which

[1] *Summa*, II. ii. 151 and 152.   [2] *De Reg. Prin.*, iv. 9.
[3] Gen. i. 28.   [4] *De Reg. Prin.*, ii. 1, 6.
[5] Troplong, *De l'Influence du Christianisme sur le Droit civil des
Romains* ; Cossa, *Guide*, p. 99 ; Devas, *Political Economy*, p. 168 ;
Périn, *La Richesse dans les Sociétés chrétiennes*, i. 541 *et seq.* ; Hettinger,
Apologie du Christianisme, v. 230 *et seq.*

work was considered to be but a form of prayer, and the manufacturer was prompted to be, not a drudge, but an artist.

In the Middle Ages, however, as we have said before, man did not exist for the sake of production, but production for the sake of man ; and wise consumption was regarded as at least as important as extended production. The high estimation in which wealth was held resulted in the elaboration of a highly developed code of regulation as to the manner in which it should be enjoyed. We do not wish to weary the reader with a repetition of that which we have already fully discussed ; it is enough to call attention to the fact that the golden mean of conduct was the observance of liberality, as distinguished, on the one hand, from avarice, or a too high estimation of material goods, and, on the other hand, from prodigality, or an undue disregard for their value. Social virtue consisted in attaching to wealth its proper value.

Far more important than its teaching either on production or consumption was the teaching of the mediæval Church on distribution, which it insisted must be regulated on a basis of strict justice. It is in this department of economic study that the teaching of the mediævals appears in most marked contrast to the teaching of the present day, and it is therefore in this department that the study of its doctrines is most valuable. As we said above, the modern world has become convinced by bitter experience of the impracticability of mere selfishness as the governing factor in distribution; and the economic thought of the time is concentrated upon devising some new system of society which shall be ruled by justice. On the one hand, we see socialists of various schools attempting to construct a Utopia in which each man shall be rewarded, not in accordance with his opportunities of growing rich at the expense of his fellow-man, but according to the services he performs; while, on the other hand, we find the Christian economists striving to induce a harassed and bewildered world to revert to an older and nobler social ethic.

It is no part of our present purpose to estimate the relative merits of these two solutions for our admittedly diseased society. Nor is it our purpose to attempt to demonstrate how far the system of economic teaching which we have sketched in the foregoing pages is applicable at the present day. We must, however, in this connection draw attention to one important consideration, namely, that the mediæval economic teaching was expressly designed to influence the only constant element in human society at every stage of economic development. Methods of production may improve, hand may give place to machine industry, and mechanical inventions may revolutionise all our conceptions of transport and communication ; but there is one element in economic activity that remains a fixed and immutable factor throughout the ages, and that element is man. The desires and the conscience of man remain the same, whatever the mechanical environment with which he is encompassed. One reason which suggests the

view that the mediæval teaching is still perfectly applicable to economic life is that it
was designed to operate upon the only factor of
economic activity that has not changed since the
Middle Ages—namely, the desires and conscience
of man.

It is important also to draw attention to the
fact that the acceptance of the economic teaching
of the mediæval theologians does not necessarily
imply acceptance of their teaching on other matters.
There is at the present day a growing body of
thinking men in every country who are full of
admiration for the ethical teaching of Christianity,
but are unable or unwilling to believe in the
Christian religion. The fact of such unbelief or
doubt is no reason for refusing to adopt the
Christian code of social justice, which is founded
upon reason rather than upon revelation, and
which has its roots in Greek philosophy and Roman
law rather than in the Bible and the writings of
the Fathers. It has been said that Christianity
is the only religion which combines religion and
ethics in one system of teaching ; but although
Christian religious and ethical teaching are combined in the teaching of the Catholic Church, they
are not inseparable. Those who are willing to
discuss the adoption of the Socialist ethic, which is
not combined with any spiritual dogmas, should
not refuse to consider the Christian ethic, which
might equally be adopted without subscribing to
the Christian dogma.

As we said above, it is no part of our intention
to estimate the relative merits of the solutions of

our social evils proposed by socialists and by Catholic economists. One thing, however, we feel bound to emphasise, and that is that these two solutions are not identical. It is a favourite device of socialists, especially in Catholic countries, to contend that their programme is nothing more than a restatement of the economic ideals of the Catholic Church as exhibited in the writings of the mediæval scholastics. We hope that the foregoing pages are sufficient to demonstrate the incorrectness of this assertion. Three main principles appear more or less clearly in all modern socialistic thought : first, that private ownership of the means of production is unjustifiable ; second, that all value comes from labour ; and, third, that all unearned income is unjust. These three great principles may or may not be sound ; but it is quite certain that not one of them was held by the mediæval theologians. In the section on property we have shown that Aquinas, following the Fathers and the tradition of the early Church, was an uncompromising advocate of private property, and that he drew no distinction between the means of production and any other kind of wealth ; in the section on just price we have shown that labour was regarded by the mediævals as but a single one of the elements which entered into the determination of value ; and in the section on usury we have shown that many forms of unearned income were not only tolerated, but approved by the scholastics.

We do not lose sight of the fact that socialism is not a mere economic system, but a philosophy, and that it is founded on a philosophical basis which conflicts with the very foundations of Christianity. We are only concerned with it here in its character of an economic system, and all we have attempted to show is that, as an economic system, it finds no support in the teaching of the scholastic writers. We do not pretend to suggest which of these two systems is more likely to bring salvation to the modern world ; we simply wish to emphasise that they are two systems, and not one. One's inability to distinguish between Christ and Barabbas should not lead one to conclude that they are really the same person.

INDEX

Consumption, regulation of, 32.
—— wise, importance of, 227.
—— wise, the aim of mediæval teaching, 223.
Contract, Thomas Aquinas on, 38.
Corinthians, Epistle to the, 48.
Corpus Juris Canonici, 13, 146.
Cossa, L., 5, 6, 17, 108, 220.
Credit, 119.
Crusades, the, influence of, 15.
—— the, influence on trade, 146.
Cunningham, Dr. W., 2, 9, 10, 11, 13, 23, 24, 26, 27, 79, 116, 122, 124, 126, 127, 128, 129, 130, 138, 139, 152, 212, 218.
Currency, *see* Money.
Cyprian, 168, 170.
—— attitude to property, 50.

DAMNUM EMERGENS, 185, 196.
—— —— nature of, 186.
—— —— universal admission of, 187.
Dante, 216.
De Regimine Principum, doubtful authorship of, 20.
Delisle, 27.
Démocratie Chrétienne, 199.
Deposit, Thomas Aquinas on, 38.
Desbuquois, Abbé, 36, 39, 104, 110, 116, 120.
Deuteronomy, 163.
Devas, 30, 49, 226.
Dictionary of Political Economy, 30, 105, 112, 135, 212.
Dictionnaire de Théologie, 45.
Didache, the, attitude to usury, 168, 170.
Diocletian rescript, regarding sales, 104.
Distribution, just, the aim of mediæval teaching, 223.
—— need for just, 31, 227.
—— regulation of, 32.
Dominicans, the, 195, 196.
Dominium eminens of the State, 69.
Donatus, 14.
Dublin Review, The, 43.
Duns Scotus, 149, 185, 188, 192.
Dureau de la Malle, 225.

Ecclesiastes, 151.
Eck, 211.
'Economic,' interpretation of, 3, 6 *et seq.*
'Economic Man,' imaginary figure conceived by classical economists, 8.

Economic Review, The, 44.
Economics, causes of lack of interest in, 14.
Elvira, the Council of, decree against usury, 169.
Emperor, the, temporal vicar of God, 11.
Encyclopaedia Britannica, The, definition of 'Middle Ages,' 4.
Endemann, 19, 20, 23, 27, 34, 108, 120, 124, 134, 151, 155, 157, 158, 177, 186, 187, 190, 191, 195, 196, 203, 204, 216, 218.
Ephesians, Epistle to the, 89.
Equality, of men, 94.
Esdras, 165.
Espinas, A., 8, 17, 163, 197, 218.
Essenes, the, and communism, 47.
Ethics, error of disregarding in economics, 29.
Eve, *see* Adam and.
Exchange, regulation of, 32.
—— justice in, 36 *et seq.*
—— theory of, see *Cambium.*
Exodus, 163.
Ezekiel, 165.

FATHERS, the, *see* Church, the early.
Favre, 173.
Feudalism, increased organisation of, in thirteenth century, 15.
Fornication, expressly forbidden by the Apostles, 168.
Franciscans, the, 195, 196.
Franciscus Patricius de Senlis, 225.
Franck, A., 20, 90, 97.
Fratricelli, the, belief in communism, 66.
Fundamentum, distinction from *titulus,* 64 *et seq.*
Funk, Dr., 113, 172, 203.

GALILEO, 159.
Gand, Henri de, 110, 149.
Garden of Eden, private property in, 55.
Gasquet, 224.
Genesis, 137, 226.
Genoa, the Archbishop of, 207.
—— —— letter from Alexander III. to, 187.
Gentile, prohibition of usury between Jew and, 164.
Gentiles, prohibition of usury not imposed on converts from, 168.
—— taking of usury from, justified, 165.

Wages, paucity of authority on, before sixteenth century, 121.

Wallon, 90, 137, 140.

Wealth, theory of, according to Aristotle, 16.

Wealth, not an end in itself 80.

Weber, 206.

William of Paris, 176.'

Wolowski, 216, 217, 221.